The Pocket Essential

BEASTIE BOYS

"People, how you doing? There's a new day dawning.
For the earth mother, it's a brand new morning.
For such a long time, there's been such a longing.
But now the sun is shining, let's roll back the awning"

'Jimmy James' – Beastie Boys

First published in Great Britain 2002 by
Pocket Essentials, P O Box 394, Harpenden, Herts, AL5 1XJ, UK

Distributed in the USA by Trafalgar Square Publishing,
PO Box 257, Howe Hill Road, North Pomfret, Vermont 05053

A CIP catalogue record for this book is available from the British Library.

ISBN 1-903047-79-X

2 4 6 8 10 9 7 5 3 1

Book typeset by Wordsmith Solutions Ltd
Printed and bound by Cox & Wyman

For Andy & Shay and Rich & Vicky –
four of my favourite people.

Acknowledgements

First up, a huge thank you to Angus Batey, author of the very excellent *Rhyming & Stealing: A History Of The Beastie Boys* who was as generous with his time as he was with his advice. Angus – you didn't have to do it (particularly since the shortage of Beastie Boys literature means that we are now arch enemies) but I'm incredibly grateful that you did. Cheers, mate.

As always, much love to my sister-in-law Emma who somehow manages to proof copy while simultaneously raising my nephew, Harry. My thanks also go to my editor Paul Duncan and my publisher Ion Mills for their patience and understanding and to John Ashbrook without whom I'd be stacking books rather than writing them.

I'd like to take this opportunity to pay tribute to the teachers who fostered my love of learning, culture and literature. So Phil Karnavas, Colin Wood, Rachel Fox, Joy Trevarthan and Andy Luck at Stanborough School, Welwyn Garden City, Professors Brian Harding and Chris Gittings at the University Of Birmingham and Professors Stephen Potts, Stephen Cox and Cynthia Walk at the University Of California, San Diego, thank you for helping me find my voice and my place in the world.

And in closing, I'd also like to doff my cap to Adam Higginbotham, Clark Collis and Damon Wise at *Neon*, Simon Crook, Matt Mueller, Cam Winstanley, Dan Jolin, Ceri Thomas and James White at *Total Film*, Emma Cochrane at *Empire* (UK), Tony Harper at *The Sun-Herald*, Ben Olins and Paul Henderson at *Hotdog*, Matt De Abaitua and Daniel Etherington at *filmfour.com*, and the team at *Empire Australia* – thanks to you, I have a passion *and* a proper job.

CONTENTS

Gratitude

How The Beastie Boys Became
The Soundtrack To My Life

There really is no reason in the world why I should be a big fan of the Beastie Boys. For one thing, I'm not a New Yorker. I'm not even an American. I was, in fact, born in Welwyn Garden City, or as it's more properly known 'Leafy' Welwyn Garden City, a frighteningly middle-class burgh in the good county of Hertfordshire, a mere twenty-five miles north of London. It's not just geography that ought to rule me out of the band-fan equation, though. Unlike the group's members, I'm neither Jewish nor a Buddhist. I only wear trainers when I'm training. I'm not into either skate- or snowboarding and I don't use phrases like "putting shame in your game" or "time to get ill" in day-to-day conversation. In fact, with my upbringing and lifestyle, I really ought to be a follower of wuss rock bands like Coldplay and Travis.

But while I do own a copy of *The Man Who* and I've a soft spot for Coldplay's 'Don't Panic,' the bulk of my CD collection is made up of hip hop releases, the vast majority of which were recorded by three nice Jewish boys from New York, New York. But why should this be? Well, for you to understand that, you're going to have to understand a few other things about me first. Aged 29 (oh all right, I've just turned 30), I'm a 16-stone, 6-foot-tall, average looking – think Orson Welles before someone introduced him to buffet dining – feature writer, critic and author whose career has reached the point where it could just about be described as successful. I've written four books. I've contributed to all my favourite magazines, I play cricket badly and rugby marginally better. I have a fair smattering of friends, a good social life and, for the most part, I'm really rather happy. Heck, if I were any more upbeat, you'd assume I was a children's TV presenter. On crack.

Unfortunately, this was not always the case. Rewind four years to the Autumn of 1998 and you'd have found a very different creature. Weighing in at a colossal 22 stones (yes, that's 22 stones – just fourteen pounds lighter than Shirley 'Big Daddy' Crabtree at his heaviest), my writing career was in such poor shape that the only work I could find was editing a department store's in-house magazine, my girth made competitive sport an impossibility and, while I did have mates, my size made me so sluggish and awkward, I invariably felt lonely and unworthy.

I suppose it's at this point of the story that I should say that I slapped on The Beastie Boys' *Check Your Head* or *Ill Communication* and my life instantly altered. But that didn't happen. What did happen was that I met two Australian rugby players. Now up until that time in my life, the Aussies I had met couldn't have impressed me less if they'd been flogging Nazi memorabilia. Brash, shallow, self-confident to the point of being arrogant – I had the same feeling towards our Southern Hemisphere cousins that I get about William Shatner when he sings. Of course, I'd never gone so far as to actually visit Australia or try and befriend any Aussies. Mine were snap judgements based on distant observations.

More fool me. Indeed, it's possible that if I hadn't been so snobbish, my life might have begun to turn around a damn sight sooner. As it was, I was 27 when I was introduced to Brett Ulrick and Brad Williams; two blokes who came to Welwyn Garden to help out the town's team and who ended up giving this boy his life back. Although they were both three years younger than me, these guys really seemed to have things sussed. An existence based on hard work both in the gym and at the office and the sort of carousing that would make the Rat Pack proud, Brett and Brad lived a life I wanted. And, more pertinently, they were generous enough to show me how to get it.

As with so many things, the solution was incredibly simple if you could summon up the odd ounce of will power because to get to where I wanted to go all I had to do was work out hard. This not only made me feel more confident but also gave me the energy to pursue my writing career more wholeheartedly and as that became more successful, so my confidence grew even more. It wasn't the sort of regime you needed a degree to understand and it wasn't stuff that I hadn't been told before. That I took the advice on board now, though, had everything to do with the fact that Brett and Brad didn't have to help me. A couple of guys passing through town, playing a bit of rugby and entertaining the good people of Welwyn Garden City, their reasons for suggesting that I alter my lifestyle were based entirely on bonhomie and it was because of this that I finally decided to put my house in order. Six months after meeting the Aussies, I was two stones lighter. One year on and I had almost completely turned the corner.

So, it wasn't in fact until after my encounter with the Australians that one of my friends at the department store I was working for, Duncan Bray, lent me a copy of the Beasties' *Paul's Boutique*. Of course, I was already aware of the Beastie Boys' work. Indeed, not only did I think that the video for 'Sabotage' was hysterical but I was a big fan of singles like 'Intergalactic' and 'Sure Shot,' and even had a grudging fondness for the stupid yet stupendous first album *Licensed To Ill*. *Paul's Boutique*, however, completely blew me away. I don't know whether it was the samples, stolen from the cream of 1970s funk and soul, the loops (if the record was any more danceable, it would need a license) or the lyrical inventiveness (it's hard not to love a band who see nothing wrong with rhyming 'Shea Stadium' with 'Varadium'), but after just one listen, I was hooked. Not long after, I owned everything the Beasties had ever recorded.

Now that I'm fully familiar with the band's output, I know exactly what it is I like about the Beastie Boys music: it's everything. I love the classy cribbing (the boys have borrowed loops from acts as diverse as Jimi Hendrix, Sly & The Family Stone, The Beatles, The Sugar Hill Gang and Steven Spielberg's composer of choice, John Williams). I love the killer cuts (it's not every act that can fully justify a 'best of' LP that runs to 42 tracks). I love the funk that's so deep you need a snorkel to survive it. I love the cheap tricks (if the boys back themselves into a corner lyrically, they'll simply spell out one of their names or start dissing one another). I love the prime rhymes, such as on 'The Negotiation Limerick File' where they ditch hip hop's standard four-line verse structure in favor of limericks that would make Edward Lear proud, as well as the rubbish ones (how can you hate performers prepared to rhyme 'commercial' with, er, 'commercial' as the fellas do on 'Pass The Mic'?). I love the fact they've made political correctness fun (it's not every act that can cram homophobia, the horror of global poverty and a homage to DC Comics into the same track – 'Alive'). I love the choice of collaborators since it doesn't matter whether the boys hook up with Q-Tip from Daisy Age rappers A Tribe Called Quest, right-wing guitar wizard Ted Nugent or reggae legend Lee 'Scratch' Perry because the relationships always work. And I love the fact that, lyrically, they've grown up

9

in public – they've gone from singing about beer and porn to giving props to Tibet and the women's movement in the space of a few short years.

As brilliant as their beats are and as inspired as the trio's delivery is, there is one thing in particular that makes the Beastie Boys' records special to me in a way that most music isn't. And what is this special ingredient? It's the fact that the band records music that proves that you can be who you want to be. Their songs almost bottle the essence of what I learnt from my Antipodean allies. Tracks like 'Sure Shot,' 'Gratitude,' 'Root Down' and 'Pass The Mic' not only celebrate the ability people have to alter their lives but serve as instruction manuals on how to effect such change. 'So this is what I've got to say to you all/be true to yourself and you will never fall' implores Mike D on *Check Your Head*'s 'Pass The Mic.' The virtues of endeavour, meanwhile, are addressed on *Ill Communication*'s 'Root Down' ('I do what I want so I never rest') and 'Sure Shot' ('Well they say I'm twenty-something and I should be slacking/but I'm working harder than ever and you can call it macking.'). Can you imagine Fred Durst doing the same thing? No, you can't. In fact, the whinging Nu Metal that's currently in vogue is the complete antithesis of the Beasties' message. Limp Bizkit's beefs about the powerlessness of youth and the fact that the only viable emotional expression is anger couldn't be more at odds with Yauch, Horovitz and Diamond's music of empowerment and enlightenment.

Of course, now that I've had my mind and horizons expanded, you might imagine the Beastie Boys no longer mean quite so much to me. Not a bit of it. Four years on from making the decision to straighten up and fly right, I still drive, work and work out to the Beasties. The thing is, the group makes you so aware that there are no restrictions on life, once you've listened to their sound and achieved immediate goals, you want to tune back in and pursue fresh challenges. So, I've still got weight I want to lose. I've still got mountains I want to climb. I've still got miles to go before I sleep. And because the Beastie Boys have shown me there really are no limits, I won't stop until I go 'Intergalactic.'

Richard Luck
Sydney, New South Wales, November 2001

In 3s

Or How The Beastie Boys Grew Up And Up And Up

It's an acknowledged fact that rock stars become less interesting the older they get. Marriages, mortgages, mewling brats: it's enough to turn even the most Satanic of hellraisers into that most meek of superheroes, Pipe 'n' Slippers Man.

Not that the onset of maturity is necessarily a bad thing. Sure, it might make you seem about as much fun as a wet weekend at Hemsby Pontins but at least it spares you the embarrassment of growing old disgracefully. Is there anything worse than someone trying to behave like Led Zeppelin at an age when they ought to be getting better acquainted with their Zimmer frame? Just look at Mick Jagger. The idea of him spending the night together with anyone is enough to make you want to call social services.

Of course, not everyone becomes increasingly bland as they become increasingly dependent on Sanatogen. Take folk legend Neil Young. Admittedly, he can no longer sing 'Keep On Rockin' In The Free World' unless he places his tongue firmly in his cheek but he remains a great performer and a wonderfully charismatic character. And then there are the Beastie Boys. Ah, yes, the Beastie Boys! The horseplay, the hi-jinks, the huge debut album: if ever you needed evidence that rock is a young man's game then the Beasties and the heat generated by *Licensed To Ill* provide it in spades. Or at least they would were it not for the fact that, fifteen years on from the day they crash-landed at the top of the American LP chart, the Beastie Boys make arguably better records, sell arguably more albums and are arguably the most revered recording act in the world today. Tonnes of people want to work with them. Everyone from Blink 182 and Limp Bizkit to The Bloodhound Gang and Papa Roach rip them off. And their promos still annually scoop the pool at the MTV Music Video Awards. Yes, Adam Horovitz (aka Adrock aka The King Adrock), Michael Diamond (aka Mike D aka Country Mike) and Adam Yauch (aka MCA aka Master Of Ceremonies Adam aka Nathaniel Hornblower) have done the impossible: they've made growing-up seem kind of cool. And that's not all they've done!

When I told my friends (okay then, friend) I was going to write a book about the Beastie Boys, the immediate reaction was: "Didn't they split up

11

ages ago?" I got the same reaction from some of my other mates (all right, people I stopped randomly in the street). I was initially a little disturbed by this but I now see how such a state of affairs could come about. When the Beasties first appeared, the media frenzy was so colossal that the failure of subsequent tours and releases to illicit the same reaction could easily lead you to think that the band had gone AWOL. It's also possible that if you don't watch music television, don't read music papers or magazines and only buy two albums a year and both of them are by The Corrs, you may well not be aware of the Beastie Boys' current whereabouts. Even if this were the case, however, your life would still be far from Beastie free. I mean, do you love Nu Metal? Well, it wouldn't exist without *Licensed To Ill*. Do you ever use the term old skool? The Beasties as good as invented the phrase. Do you have concerns about the troubles of Tibet? Well, you probably wouldn't know too much about China's atrocities had the band not dedicated so much time and money to raising awareness. And is the VW sign missing from the front of your motor? Yep, there's no denying it: it's a Beastie universe.

And what a strange world it is that the Beasties inhabit, a place where weird coincidence and strange luck coexist with peculiar contradictions and perplexing paradoxes. For only on Planet Beastie would i) the decision to turn your back on the music that made you millionaires be deemed sensible because it aided the progression of the band's sound, ii) the choosing of three blokes you met at a party to produce your difficult second album turn out to be a master stroke, and iii) the idea of keeping your carpenter on the payroll because of his keyboard skills seem to make perfect sense.

Even the band's name has contradictory qualities. For one thing, the Beastie Boys used to have a girl member. For another, these boys aren't beasts, they're blue bloods. Indeed, Adam Horovitz might have been born in West Orange, New Jersey, on 31 October 1966 but he was raised in Manhattan by his father Israel, the award-winning playwright behind such works as *Lebensraum, Line* and *Scrooge & Marley: A Christmas Carol*. While he certainly didn't want for money or material possessions, things were actually pretty tough for Horovitz from the get go. Crippled by leg problems that were never properly diagnosed and from which he has never fully recovered, Adam H also had to endure the pain of watching his mother drink herself to death. Doris Horovitz would die from alcoholism while Adam was still in his early teens. It says a lot for Adrock that he was able to cope with these traumas. His siblings also successfully overcame their bereavement. His sister Rachael went on to produce David Mamet's big-screen adaptation of *State & Main* while brother Matthew has worked as an author and actor.

Mike Diamond shared Horovitz's privileged upbringing if not his childhood misfortune. The son of art dealer parents, Mike was born on Manhattan Island on 20 November 1965. Like Adam Yauch, born in Brooklyn on 5 August 1964 to an architect father, Diamond's upbringing was well heeled but unremarkable to the extent that almost nothing is known about him prior to his starting to dick around with John Berry, Kate Schellenbach and Jeremy Shatten (respectively, the Stuart Sutcliffe, Pete Best and Tommy Moore of the Beasties' story). Known as The Young Aboriginals, it's hard to take this early musical venture too seriously since the group only played two concerts before splitting up and both of these were on the same night. Renaming themselves the Beastie Boys, the group brought in Yauch to replace Shatten on bass duties and started playing gigs across the five boroughs.

It's perhaps important to point out that, at this stage, the Beasties weren't a rap/hip hop act. During their first three years together, the group played almost exclusively hardcore punk rock. That they happened to play it pretty appallingly didn't bother the band in the slightest since the Beasties had got together to have a good time rather than to make great music. And so for a few glorious years, the Beastie Boys (Beastie being an acronym for Boys Entering Anarchistic States Towards Internal Excellence, according to Mike D) played the odd gig, drank too many beers, split up a couple of times and generally acted the goat.

Things only changed when someone offered the band a recording contract. True, the contract was literally for one record and was proffered by record shop owner Dave Parsons but it gave the group the opportunity to be immortalised on vinyl. By the time the 'Polly Wog Stew' EP emerged, however, Berry had decided to call it a day. Enter Adam Horovitz, late of a hardcore band that rejoiced in the name of The Young & The Useless.

It was around this time that the Beastie Boys started experimenting with hip hop. Like a lot of white school kids at the time, the band were aware of what rap was but while their Caucasian classmates were sworn off such 'devil music,' the Beasties as a band and Mike D in particular embraced

13

both the sound and the culture. The group's attempts to incorporate hip hop into their repertoire were clumsy at first and tended to piss off their hardcore audiences (the Beasties had a poor reputation amongst hardcore purists as it was since they weren't thought to take punk rock seriously enough). It wasn't long, however, before the band had laid down a track that had the rap community licking its lips.

'Cookie Puss' (or 'Cooky Puss' as it was called on the record sleeve) was basically a series of crank phone calls made to Tom Carvel's ice cream company, the makers of the most salubriously monikered confectionary this side of the Walnut Whip, relayed over some rudimentary break beats. Hear it now and you won't understand what all the fuss was about but at the time had 'Cookie Puss' been any hotter, it would have gone supernova. Also of interest was the B-side 'Beastie Revolution' which, according to one version of events, became the subject of legal proceedings when it was used without permission in a British Airways advertisement. BA, so the Beasties' story goes, wound up having to pay the band $40,000 which they used to prolong their lifestyle of singing and slacking. That no such case can be found in law books on either side of the Atlantic suggests it's quite possibly a figment of the group's collective imagination that, in turn, reveals one of the major problems in writing a history of the Beastie Boys. The group lies. A lot.

What is for certain is that within a couple of years of taking/not taking BA for a huge sum of money, the Beastie Boys were sitting on a considerably bigger pile of cash. Now signed to Russell Simmons' ultra-hip Def Jam label, the band, minus the recently departed Schellenbach, began working on an album that would change the face of hip hop forever. 1986's *Licensed To Ill* proved that not only could white men shake their rump but that rap music was capable of conquering the American chart. Admired by everyone from the legendary Grandmaster Flash to the ever so right-on *Village Voice*, the reaction to the record couldn't have been more different to the reaction to the band. A bunch of witless arseholes who had either got lucky or sold their souls, in the eyes of the music press, the media and the silent majority, the Beastie Boys couldn't have been more reprehensible if they peddled child porn. The kids, of course, adored them. And so it was the Beastie Boys set off on an amazing adventure, touring the world, raking in the money and upsetting as many people as possible. And when they realised that moneymaking and pissing folks off wasn't all that it was cracked up to be, they went into hiding.

F Scott Fitzgerald said that there are no second acts in American lives. Karl Marx, clearly no fan of *The Great Gatsby*, disagreed, stating that: "All great events and personalities in world history reappear... the second time as farce." That the Beastie Boys contradicted the authors of *Tender Is The Night* and *The Communist Manifesto* isn't to suggest they boast superior intellects but it does say something about their powers of reinvention. For far from being a farce, the Beasties' second American life was musically flawless. Not that this second album, *Paul's Boutique*, was a financial success. In fact, it took so long to make, cost so much to record and sold so slowly, the group was almost dropped by their new record company Capitol. Then, after a lengthy cooling off period, the band produced a third LP, *Check Your Head*, the sales of which proceeded to go through the roof. Come albums four and five, *Ill Communication* and *Hello Nasty*, and the Beastie Boys were again selling records on a scale that the managers of even the most successful boy bands would envy. Just what the bloody hell was going on?

From everywhere to nowhere to everywhere again, the Beasties' success story hasn't been straightforward. As with all journeys of conquest, however, there has been a degree of empire building, culminating in the creation of the band's record label cum magazine publisher cum clothing company Grand Royal. In coming back from the brink to becoming bigger than ever, the band has also assembled a small army of associates. Of their many lieutenants, none has perhaps had as much influence over the group as Mario G Caldato Junior. A recording engineer of Brazilian extraction, Caldato was introduced to the boys when they were recording *Paul's Boutique* and has co-produced all their subsequent LPs. A good friend to Messrs Yauch, Horovitz and Diamond (yes, I know it sounds like a law firm), Caldato has such an understanding of the group's music he has salvaged more than one track with his ability to improvise. Indeed, the way he picked the superb 'The Negotiation Limerick File' off the studio floor and turned it into one of the standout tracks on *Hello Nasty*. This should be reason enough for a sub-editor to entitle a Beastie's article 'Super Mario's Band.'

Besides helping the boys' sound evolve, Caldato also introduced the Beasties to a tradesman who is second to none. Mark Ramos Nishita had been friends with Mario C since school. He entered the Beasties' universe when there was an accident at the place the boys were renting during the *Paul's Boutique* sessions and Nishita, a qualified carpenter, was called in to repair a post. When Yauch and Co. found out that Nishita went by the nickname of Keyboard Money Mark the group asked him how he got his moniker and he happily showed them. He has since become such a fixture that he was even billed alongside the three regular band members on *Check Your Head*. As for the rest of the Beastie brigade, it's rounded out by DJs Hurricane and Mix Master Mike, percussionist Eric Bobo (who takes time off from his regular act Cypress Hill to work with the Beasties), heavyweight rapper Biz Markie, backing vocalist Brooke Williams and many of the artists signed to Grand Royal. Of course, the group doesn't require a legion to fight any battles: they need one to help them make the best music possible. There was a time, however, when fighting was something the Beastie Boys did pretty much all of the time.

For those that didn't live through it, it's hard to grasp just how big a stink the Beastie Boys kicked up when they first hit big. If their lyrics about guns, hos and drink and lascivious videos weren't bad enough, the boys had an X-rated stage show and an interview technique that was confrontational to say the least. They also possessed possibly the stupidest gimmick in the entire history of hip hop. As a pisstake/homage to the likes of LL Cool J and Run DMC who were prone to wearing thick gold chains, Mike Diamond had taken to sporting the chain from a toilet around his neck to which he had attached the emblem from a VW auto. It was an utterly ridiculous piece of paraphernalia and Mike knew it but as soon as the fans saw what their hero was wearing, no Volkswagen in the world was safe. Even now you can probably find battered old VWs with gaping holes where the company insignia ought to be. Back in 1987, the problem became so big that car dealers were asking Volkswagen to supply them with extra emblems so that they could give them away to teenagers in an attempt to stop the rot. While it might have seemed funny at the time, the VW badge-phenomenon probably did as much harm to the Beasties' image as anything. To sing about bad behaviour was one thing. But to encourage kids to damage something as sacred as a man's car... they may as well have raped the Pope.

The other unforgivable thing the band did was to ridicule a bunch of terminally ill children at the Montreux Rock Festival. Well, at least, that's what British tabloid the *Daily Mirror* alleged they did. According to the Beasties and the people looking after the kids no such incident took place but it was this story that ran on the front cover of a newspaper with 2 million readers and it was this indiscretion, be it fictitious or otherwise, that primed all right-thinking people in Britain to give the Beastie Boys a tough time during their tour of the country.

What made things even worse for the band was the way they handled the attention and the antagonism. Instead of placating the press and the public a little by toning their act down, the boys made sure Great Britain got the Beasties at their most obnoxious. This meant behaving excessively boor-ishly on stage and flicking V-signs and acting in a generally surly manner in interviews. Okay, so they never quite matched the Sex Pistols' behaviour during their infamous confrontation with Bill Grundy. But if you wanted evidence of the Beasties' lack of maturity around the time of *Licensed To Ill*, you needed to look no further than the way they handled themselves on the Raising Hell tour. Of course, it was perhaps too much to expect the boys to behave in any manner other than immaturely – they were all in their early twenties at the time of the visit – but while their sophomoric antics guaran-teed that they got more press coverage than Run DMC, technically the tour's headlining band, they also made certain that the Beasties couldn't tour Britain or pretty much any other place for the best part of five years.

Fastforward ten years to the Reading Festival and arguably the Beastie Boys' second most famous controversy. Topping the bill with The Prodigy, the Beasties, or more specifically Adam Yauch, took issue with one of the tracks the Essex dance legends intended to play, 'Smack My Bitch Up.' As MCA would explain to *The O-Zone*: "I have a girl friend who has been in abusive relationships and she said: 'Every time I hear that song, I want to be sick.'" Since it was one of the highlights of their smash hit LP *The Fat Of The Land* and none of the Beasties' business really, The Prodigy told MCA and Co. to get stuffed and included 'Smack My Bitch Up' in their set any-way.

Depending upon which music paper you read, the falling out between the bands reached the scale of either a short but heated argument or a bar-room brawl. Whatever the truth, it's important to point out that what was being argued over at Reading was somewhat more important than the Manic Street Preachers and Billy Bragg bickering over toilet facilities at Glastonbury. Over the years, the Beasties have substantially toned down the violent content of their tracks. MCA: "When I realised that lyrics really do affect people, I thought more about what I was putting out into the world." All they were doing at the festival was suggesting that another influential band ought to follow suit. Rather like a good history teacher, I can see both sides of the argument since I love the track in question but hate violence towards women (not a particularly controversial position that second one, I know, but one that I think we should all adopt). And also like an historian, I'm now able to see that the band didn't come to blows, rather they came to that most adult of opinions, they simply agreed to disagree. The Beastie Boys argued that if The Prodigy respected them as artists (given that *The Fat Of The Land* featured a track, 'Funky Shit,' which contained a sample from *Ill Communication*'s 'Root Down,' it's safe to assume they did), they should respect their opinion on this issue. And The Prodigy's Liam Howlett pointed out that the Beasties might not have been in the best position to comment by cheekily sampling the line 'If I played guitar, I'd be Jimmy Page/The girlies I like are underage' from the boys' 'The New Style' on his *Dirt Chamber Sessions* album.

From brawling and bawling to talking things through like men, the Beastie Boys have certainly changed a lot. Besides losing the references to guns and bitches (I wonder if Axl Rose ever considered calling his band that!), Adam Yauch, as he explained to *Bomb* magazine, is now so high on life, he hardly ever uses dope anymore: "Except for every once in a while, I've pretty much stopped smoking herb. These days, I'm trying to achieve those states of mind through meditation. It helps me keep a clear perspective and be more in control – as opposed to getting launched into some shit and going 'Whoa! Where the fuck am I?'" With the Beasties, though, it isn't so much a case of 'just say no' as 'just say know.' Indeed, what makes the Beastie Boys remarkable is that, while going through the process of growing up, they haven't grown old. Sure, the boys all got married (Horovitz to Donovan's daughter the actress Ione Skye, Diamond to film director Tamra Davis and Yauch to Dechen Wangdu) but you can rest assured that they screwed around plenty before realising that, as the American comedian Dennis Miller puts it, "married life gives you the longest string of one night stands ever." The band also seems to realise that responsibility ain't a bad thing as with it comes money and power, two things that young people rarely get a sniff of. Being young isn't actually that great since you don't have the experience to appreciate life nor the influence or financial clout to alter it. As the Beastie Boys prove, being older, wiser and richer is much better.

The combination of staying young but becoming responsible hasn't curtailed the Beasties' relevance, as becomes blatantly apparent when you look at how the band continues to shape contemporary culture. In 1998, German boy band NYCC's cover of 'Fight For Your Right' was a hit the length and breadth of Europe. That, as covers go, it was down there with Maria Carey and Westlife's massacring of Phil Collins' 'Against All Odds' is by the by. What was important, nay even revelatory, was that a song written over a decade earlier and pretty much disowned by its creators could still connect with pop kids. The Beasties also continue to crop up in the strangest of places: kicking in a loungecore instrumental version of 'Start' for the Jam tribute CD *Fire & Skill*, providing the backing for the 'Skills To Pay The Bills' ball juggling strand on Sky Sports' *Soccer AM*, doing battle with the Backstreet Boys in the claymation chaos that is MTV's *Celebrity Death Match* and lending their vocal talents to 'Hell Is Other Robots,' an episode of Matt Groening's underrated sci-fi comedy *Futurama*.

To find out where the Beastie Boys carry the most clout, you have to look at that which has done the most to keep them young: the music. Over the course of their five LPs, the Beasties have tried their hand at countless styles and genres. Indeed, listen to the group's later albums, principally *Hello Nasty*, and you could be forgiven for thinking you're hearing a highly eclectic compilation LP. Whether they're lifting their beats from a smoke-filled jazz club or the souped-up romper room that passes for their G-Son recording facility, the Beasties never fall short of kicking serious arse. Thanks to them, the scratch wheel now sounds as familiar to music lovers as the snare drum, samples are as every day as axe licks and sudden shifts in style feel as cosy as the acoustic guitar. Furthermore, the group has proven that pushing the envelope isn't just the musical equivalent of the high school dare, it's essential if you're to locate the greatest tunes and so discover where the true glory lies. Now, there are loads of great artists but how many of them ever really experiment? Push the envelope? Shit, most of these guys don't even own any stationery. The Beastie Boys, on the other hand, reinvent the wheel more times than most people sneeze.

And what is the upshot of the boys evolving a highly sophisticated noise culture, proving that rap can be the domain of the white man and showing that bands should never be frightened of adopting new methods, manners or political positions? It's influence on an almost immeasurable scale. Because if it wasn't for the Beastie Boys, you wouldn't have Moby sampling early twentieth-century black music on *Play*. You wouldn't have Beck borrowing loops from classical music, ancient bluegrass LPs and obscure funk tracks on *Odelay*. You wouldn't have the Fun Lovin' Criminals closing out *100% Columbian* with a radio commercial for a limousine company or UNKLE building an album track around an ad for the ancient children's game Ball Buster. You wouldn't have the brilliant Aspects, a British hip hop duo whose debut work won immediate comparisons with the Beasties' *Paul's Boutique*. You wouldn't have the Moog-heavy movie soundtracks of David Holmes. You wouldn't have samples cropping up on everything from heavy metal tracks to numbers by boy bands like Five and N'Sync. You wouldn't have guitar groups like Northern Ireland's Ash taking to the stage with scratch DJs. In fact, you wouldn't have any DJ culture to speak of at all so there'd be no Fatboy Slim, no Bentley Rhythm Ace, no Chemical Brothers, no Daft Punk, no Gorrilaz, no Handsome Boy Modelling School and no Basement Jaxx. You'd also have no Nu Metal which would mean no Limp Bizkit, no Bloodhound Gang, no Blink 182, no Linkin Park and no Alien Ant Farm. There'd be no unlikely crossovers like Puff Daddy working with the Foo Fighters, The Wu-Tang Clan's Redman hooking up with The Off-spring or Texas working with the Clan's Method Man. And you wouldn't have the biggest current act in the world Marshall Mathers III, aka Eminem. Basically, without the Beastie Boys you wouldn't have anything. Nothing worthwhile at any rate.

Yes, this is the story of the Beastie Boys and, believe me, you won't believe it. But how does one tell such as incredible tale? To begin with, I'll look at each of the band's five albums in detail while also passing an eye over their EPs and compilation releases. Then I'll take a look at the Beasties' video work, their flirtation with movies, their charitable enterprises, the rise and fall of their record label and the phenomenon that is the Beastie Boys on tour. But before we can do any of this, in order to fully appreciate the importance of the Beasties, I'm afraid we first have to take a look at something very, very horrible indeed...

Great White Tripe

A Brief History Of Caucasians In Rap Music

If you ever need to assemble a list of popular music atrocities, you really only need to look at the disasters that happen when white people dabble in hip hop. There's PJ & Duncan ('So many rhymes we're frightened to use them' – of course you are, lads), DJ Sven and MC Miker G (remember, drugs are legal in Holland), House Of Pain (the Tommy Boy signings who made a big deal about being Irish-Americans despite the fact that their DJ was from Latvia and the other members of the band were about as Irish as Yoko Ono), Vanilla Ice (whose real name is Rob Van Winkle and who now hosts a programme on the appalling Granada's Men & Motors), Marky Mark (how fortunate it was for us all that Mark Wahlberg turned out to be such a good actor), Snow (what exactly is a 'boom boom' and why, for that matter, would you want to lick it down?)... do I need to go on?

What makes awful white rap acts like these all the more depressing is the fact that the subgenre got off to such an impressive start. While not technically a rap record, Blondie's 'Rapture' (which reached the top five in the UK in 1981 and was a number one hit in the US) had impeccable hip hop credentials. Not only did the song namecheck awesome rap innovator Fab Five Freddy but the great man actually appeared in the video as did highly-regarded alternative artist Jean-Michel Basquiat. If giving props to all the right people wasn't enough, 'Rapture' also featured the awesome Debbie Harry who handled the rhyming a lot better than anyone had any reason to expect her to and who looked absolutely drop-dead gorgeous in the video (we were talking about that promo in the playground at my school for weeks).

Quite how we got from the lofty heights of 'Rapture' to George Michael and Andrew Ridgeley mincing their way through 'Wham Rap' is hard to say. The problem was that it wasn't until acts like Run DMC came along that anyone was willing to take rap seriously. MTV even went so far as to ban hip hop music which is pretty amazing when you consider that in 2001 the station's most popular offshoot was their 24-hour rap and R&B channel. With such limited exposure, rap remained a novelty and it was for that reason that white people who should have known better were allowed to toy with a form they had absolutely no understanding of.

So where were the saviours of Caucasian rap going to come from? Strange as it might seem, for a short while it looked like Vanilla Ice might be the white knight the subgenre was looking for. This Vanilla Ice isn't the man who sold out to SBK Records for $1.5m on the understanding that he would dilute his hip hop stylings with a distinctive pop sound, however. No, this is the pre-purgatory Ice, a Miami-born but Dallas-raised kid who was so talented an MC, Public Enemy's Chuck D, was happy to tour with the young man and even considered signing him up. "If there was going to be an Elvis of rap," D explained on Channel 4's *The Hip Hop Years*, "I thought he might as well be on my label." Had Vanilla Ice stayed true to himself and his sound, we might still be talking about him positively today. As it is, once his conversion to pop star was complete, the Ice Man melted quicker than a Popsicle on a midsummer Texan afternoon.

Of course, in the years following the Rob Van Winkle debacle, some good white rappers emerged. NWA founder and Eminem's unearther Dr Dre was particularly outspoken in his support for former House Of Pain front man Everlast. However, if you were to ask someone to name killer Caucasian MCs from the late 1980s and early 1990s, it's quite possible that the list would only feature the names Mike Diamond and the Adams Horovitz and Yauch. While Adam Y was particularly well thought of in the hip hop community, all of the Beastie Boys enjoyed respect on a level that Snow could only dream of. They didn't get it immediately, mind. While *Licensed To Ill* was largely lorded, the group had to handle a number of novelty act accusations and because of the record's heavy metal orientation, some even refused to acknowledge them as a proper hip hop act. No, it wasn't until *Paul's Boutique* was released that people took the Beastie Boys completely seriously. And it wasn't until *Check Your Head* impressively debuted on the album chart that the group was considered not only the godfathers of white rap, but arguably the finest hip hop act in the world.

Nowadays, no one is that surprised to see white rap acts like Eminem and hip hop influenced Nu Metal outfits like Limp Bizkit selling out stadiums and shifting units. That these artists enjoy the success they do has everything to do with the Beastie Boys, however. I mean, imagine if white rappers had only Vanilla Ice to look up to for inspiration? The genre would be as dead as the dinosaurs.

It's some measure of the boys' power and the crucial role they played in freeing up white people so that they could play with the machinery of hip hop that no one batted an eyelid when the group received props in the video for Rage Against The Machine's cover of Afrika Bambaataa and The Soul Sonic Force's 'Renegades Of Funk,' this in spite of the fact that every other act that was paid homage to was black. Then again, the fact that you've got a predominantly white act like RATM covering hip hop classics (their recent *Renegades* tribute album also featured killer reworkings of Eric B & Rakim's 'Microphone Fiend' and Run DMC's 'I'm Housin'') is largely down to Yauch, Horovitz & Diamond: three men whose skill and success have not just enabled us to forget the early embarrassing history of white rap but made hip hop a truly colour blind art form.

The Young & The Useless

It's rather appropriate that after talking about a dreadful genre, we should now discuss the Beastie Boys' darkest hour musically. Hardcore is something that never fully caught on in the UK, largely because it seems to have been an American response to the fact that, while the US created punk, their acts were never quite as good at it as British bands like The Sex Pistols, The Clash and The Stranglers.

Characterised by guitar playing that was only marginally slower than the breakneck speed vocals and a rhythm section that clearly had little understanding of its job description, there were admittedly some quite good hardcore bands. Black Flag are a case in point, although it's worth remembering that they did have the then 21-year-old Henry Rollins in their corner – even without his muscle definition and his tattoos, the young Henry boasted a massive voice and awesome stage presence. Other acts such as the Washington-founded but New York City-based Bad Brains and the wonderfully named Reagan Youth were more of an acquired taste.

Bad Brains, however, were the band the first incarnation of the Beastie Boys wanted to be and it was covers of Bad Brains songs together with other genre favourites and a few numbers of their own that comprised the Beasties' early repertoire. If their heroes sounded rough and ready, then Schellenbach, Yauch, Diamond and Berry came on like they had been residing in a dumpster. Lyrically pretty formidable ('Fuck the chickens I don't like milk/fuck the chickens I don't like milk' rant the boys on 'Michelle's Farm'), the words nevertheless sounded like the work of Lennon & McCartney next to the sub-Pistols thrash that posed for music. The Beastie Boys are to be admired for the fact that they've never pretended to be able to play their instruments. One listen to their early stuff and you'll appreciate that there isn't a hint of false modesty about this statement.

Just as only a real devotee would hunt down woeful Warsaw bootleg cassettes so they could say they were a real Joy Division fan, so the Beasties' debut recordings are so shoddy there really is no reason for the casual listener to feel obliged to track them down. If, however, you feel you must familiarise yourself fully with the boys' oeuvre, save yourself hours traipsing around the second-hand record shops of Notting Hill or Nagoya and instead get your mits on...

'Polly Wog Stew' EP (1982, Ratcage)

Producer: Dave Parsons

Track Listing: 'Beastie Boys,' 'Transit Cops,' 'Jimi,' 'Holy Snappers,' 'Riot Fight,' 'Ode To...,' 'Michelle's Farm,' 'Egg Raid On Mojo'

In Brief: What happens when four New York kids try to emulate bands that were about as worth trying to emulate as The Skids. Or Generation X, for that matter.

The Beef: Of the eight tracks on 'Polly Wog Stew,' the only one of real note is 'Egg Raid On Mojo' which reappeared albeit in drastically different (i.e. far superior) form on *Paul's Boutique* as 'Eggman.' As for the other stuff here, it's probably fine if you like this sort of thing. And if you do like this sort of thing, please write to me care of Pocket Essentials to explain the attraction because I don't think I could uncover it with a metal detector.

Incidentally, 'Polly Wog Stew' was recorded over the course of a single weekend. You'd never have guessed!

The Verdict: While it's quite awe-inspiring that 'Polly Wog Stew' ever got released, you also have to admire the listener who is able to listen to it the whole way through. 1/5

And you don't even have to dine on 'Polly Wog Stew' now that the band have released...

Some Old Bullshit (1994, Grand Royal)

Catalogue Number: EST 2877 (CD EST 89843)

Producers: Various Artists

Track Listing: 'Egg Raid On Mojo (4 Track),' 'Beastie Boys,' 'Transit Cops,' 'Jimi,' 'Holy Snappers,' 'Riot Fight,' 'Ode To...,' 'Michelle's Farm,' 'Egg Raid On Mojo,' 'Transit Cops (4 track),' 'Cookie Puss,' 'Bonus Batter,' 'Beastie Revolution,' 'Cookie Puss (Censored Version)'

In Brief: A compilation of the band's doodlings from what we shall from now on refer to as 'the difficult years,' this contains 'Polly Wog Stew' in its entirety, together with both the censored and banned versions of 'Cookie Puss' which is clearly the comedy record equivalent of the joke you had to be there at the time to find amusing.

The Beef: Some Old Bullshit has little to recommend it other than that it was released in an effort to save fans in general and completionists in particular their hard-earned cash. As Mike D explains in the album's sleeve notes: "As time went on, the 'Polly Wog Stew' 7 inch became unavailable as did the 'Cookie Puss' 12 inch, replaced by import-only CDs and cassettes. So finally, it seemed like a good time to try and make this stuff available together in one joint for a reasonable sum." It's just a shame the music can't be applauded in quite the same way as the gesture.

The Verdict: The most appropriately entitled record this side of Ronan Keating's 'You Say It Best When You Say Nothing At All.' 1/5

Of course, there are other Beastie releases available from this era and you could probably fork out a lot of cash to lay your hands on them. But, please – save your money. And save both you and me the hassle of having to contemplate this miserable period in the musical development of the band by scampering on quickly to the next chapter.

Beastie Revolution

Despite the cult success of 'Cookie Puss,' it's unlikely that the Beastie Boys would have amounted to very much had they not lost the services of John Berry (who quit to work with Thwig and Big Fat Love, whom he had on the go at the time and with whom he still performs), recruited Adam Horovitz full time and gained access to the production and management skills of Rick Rubin and Russell Simmons. Originally brought on to Def Jam's staff in 1984, the group was initially employed as A&R men. Adrock even had a big hand in discovering LL Cool J. During their first two years with the company, the band cut just one disk, the flop single 'Rock Hard.' The Def Jam connection alas eventually led to Kate Schellenbach being painted into a corner but it also secured the band their first taste of single success with 1986's sneering, sexed up 'She's On It' taken from the soundtrack to the movie *Krush Groove*, itself a Def Jam production (see Beastly Movies). As unpleasant and excellent as this debut track was, it couldn't prepare the world for what the Beastie/Rubin/Simmons axis would release next...

Licensed To Ill (1986, Def Jam)

Catalogue Number: Def Jam 4500621

Producers: Rick Rubin and The Beastie Boys

Track Listing: 'Rhymin' & Stealin'' 'The New Style,' 'She's Crafty,' 'Posse In Effect,' 'Slow Ride,' 'Girls,' 'Fight For Your Right,' 'No Sleep Till Brooklyn,' 'Paul Revere,' 'Hold It Now, Hit It,' 'Brass Monkey,' 'Slow And Low,' 'Time To Get Ill'

In Brief: Three nice Jewish boys from the better boroughs of New York come on like horny, drunken hooligans then try to pretend it's all an act. Yeah, right!

The Origins: The Beasties' shift from hardcore punk to rap struck most critics as strange and made many reviewers suspicious. The popular belief was that the group had cashed in their credibility for short-term fame. Rick Rubin, however, believed the switch from one style to another made perfect sense. It was, after all, a jump he himself had made. As a hardcore-loving university student, Rubin realised that the form had its limitations. Because of this and because he saw the same energy in rap as in hardcore, he began hanging out with NYU's black clique through which he became friends with Russell Simmons.

If anyone ever tells you the American Dream is a fascist fantasy, you could do worse than drop the name of Russell Simmons. A black kid raised in utter poverty, Simmons got himself out of New York's roughest districts through a combination of self-education, confidence and wheeler dealing. His many coups included managing his brother's rap act, Run DMC, launching his own record label, Def Jam, going into film production and creating the hugely successful HBO black showcase *Russell Simmons' Def Comedy Jam.*

Of course, Russell wouldn't have got anywhere without an eye for talent and it was this that brought both Rubin and the Beasties into his orbit. Still a metal freak at heart, Rubin suggested that the boys bolster their hip hop sound with heavy Led Zeppelin-esque guitars and drumming, even going so far as to sample Jon Bonham's tub thumping. Rubin also fostered the Beasties' incendiary stage performances. Convinced that the purpose of rock 'n' roll music was to piss off your parents as much as possible, he encouraged the Beasties to behave like complete basket cases. Indeed, if Malcolm McLaren had been born in America, liked heavy metal music and had been able to grow his hair long he might have been Rick Rubin. Rubin's comments in Alex Ogg's superb *The Hip Hop Years* certainly invite such a comparison: "At the time the Beasties broke they were perceived like The Sex Pistols – outrageous, rude, outlaw, snotty, arrogant. And not talented. They were as hated as they were loved. People would always say to me that when they had success they were such jerks and assholes. But that's what they were always like. It's not the success that made them miserable, they were just kinda obnoxious and that's what made them who they were. They always thought they were the greatest thing in the world before they ever sold one record." But once their first full-length record was out, it was apparent that the Beasties' arrogance might have some basis in fact.

The Standout Track: 'Fight For Your Right.' In general, I've chosen the best number on each album as the Standout Track but while 'Fight For Your Right' can't hold a candle to 'She's Crafty,' 'The New Style' or 'Hold It Now, Hit It' musically, it captured the mid-1980s Zeitgeist so perfectly, it would be churlish not to talk about it in depth.

Amazingly, the record had not been earmarked for a 7-inch release. "'Slow Ride' was the single," Russell Simmons told Alex Ogg. "I think they made 'Fight For Your Right' more to have a good time and as a joke. They weren't thinking that this was going to be something that defines their career. It did not sound like the rest of the album." Simmons is right – 'Fight For Your Right' does stand out from the rest of *Licensed To Ill*. A conventional rock song in a sea of hip hop, it, nevertheless, remains true to the spirit of the LP and features the souped-up guitar and *South Park*-style bawling that are the album's signatures. Could the world exist without, 'Fight For Your Right'? Absolutely. Is the world different because it does exist? Very.

The Prime Rhyme: Most groups take a couple of albums to get songwriting licked. Even Neil Finn's earliest recordings contain their fair share of naïve crap. The Beastie Boys, however, had the measure of hip hop from day one. On *Licensed To Ill*, they were even doing things as ambitious as creating their own mythology (to wit: 'Paul Revere' – 'Here's a little story I've got to tell/about three bad brothers you know so well/it started way back in history/With Adrock, MCA and me, Mike D.'). On songs like 'She's Crafty,' meanwhile, the well-brought-up Manhattanites had great fun pretending to be whore fuckers – 'I think her name is Lucy but they all call her Loose/I think I thought I seen her on eighth and forty-deuce/The next thing she said: 'my place or yours?/Let's kick some bass behind closed doors.'' However, since *Licensed To Ill*'s raison d'être was to upset people, the gold medal has to go to the aforementioned controversy-stoking 'The New Style' – that line one more time, 'If I played guitar I'd be Jimmy Page/The girlies I like are underage.'

The Cover: One of the most celebrated album sleeves of the 1980s, the cover of *Licensed To Ill* features a painting of an engorged jumbo jet with a Beasties logo on its tailfin. Possibly intended as a reference to Led Zeppelin's infamous pleasure palace in the sky, the sleeve has attained legendary status on account of it having two stings in its tail. The first is that, when you fold the sleeve out, you see that the plane has in fact run directly into a cliff. Meanwhile, if you check out the jumbo's flight number in a mirror you'll find that it reads 'EAT ME.'

Influenced By: It's fair to say there would be no *Licensed To Ill* were it not for Joseph Simmons, Darryl McDaniels and Jason Mizell, aka Run

DMC. With their porkpie hats, unlaced Adidas trainers, thick-rimmed glasses and adverts for The Gap, Run DMC has begun to resemble a panto-mime act. But while they might not know when to call it quits (2001's *Crown Royal* was a truly tragic collection of tired remixes and woeful new material), there's no denying the role the group played in taking hip hop from the back streets of the Bronx into the homes of music lovers the world over.

To tell the full, unexpurgated story of Run DMC, you'd need a book every bit as long as this one but if it's the impact the band had upon the Beastie Boys you're interested in, you need look no further than the *Raising Hell* album. Having enjoyed success with their previous LP, *King Of Rock*, which was a million seller in the US, McDaniels (DMC), Simmons (Run) and Mizell (Jam Master Jay) were instructed by their manager, Run's brother Russell, to work with Rick Rubin. Just as he later did with the Beasties, Rubin set about beefing up Run DMC's sound. This involved hav-ing the rappers sing over sampled guitar riffs. For example, the track 'It's Tricky' featured cut-ups from The Knack's 'My Sharona' and Toni Basil's 'Oh Mickey.' Rubin's methods did not initially play too well with the trio. Darryl McDaniels was particularly ticked off when the producer suggested that the group record a cover version of Aerosmith's 'Walk This Way.' The group already knew of the track since they'd been styling over the drumbeat introduction from day one but the idea of recording a rock song was anath-ema to a rap act. And as for the idea of actually bringing in Steve Tyler and Joe Perry to perform 'Walk This Way' with them, you might as well have asked McDaniels and Co. to sing something by The Smurfs. The track, however, did get recorded and preceded to blow up big time, transforming Run DMC from America's biggest rap act, which was then the equivalent of being the most popular poet in Milton Keynes, to global stars.

Run DMC did more than test-drive a sound for the Beastie Boys. Besides bringing MTV around to the idea that rap music might actually have an audience, McDaniels, Simmons and Mizell gave the boys a support slot on their Raising Hell tour and even helped out on a couple of tracks on *Licensed To Ill* (see Collaborators & Cohorts). Being a band that places a high price on loyalty, the Beasties have never forgotten what their friends did for them and have tried to repay the favour whenever and wherever possible, even risking their credibility by contributing to the *Crown Royal* fiasco!

Influences On: You might be able to exist without Nu Metal, aka the Nu Stoopid, but Nu Metal certainly couldn't exist without *Licensed To Ill*. To be fair, the genre's better performers readily acknowledge the importance of the Beasties' release. "We were huge fans," remarked The Bloodhound Gang's Jimmy Pop on MTV2, "right up to the point where they started hanging out with the Dalai Lama." Not that the Beasties' religious posturing stopped Pop's outfit from ransacking *Licensed To Ill* wholesale for their own highly entertaining LPs *One Fierce Beer Coaster* and *Hooray For Boobies*. (*Hooray*'s 'The Inevitable Return Of The Great White Dope' and 'Three Point One Four' clearly owe huge debts to 'No Sleep Till Brooklyn' and 'She's Crafty.') You can also hear echoes of *Licensed To Ill* in Blink 182's *Enema Of The State*, Alien Ant Farm's cover of Michael Jackson's 'Smooth Criminal' and the music of Linkin Park, Papa Roach and Australia's very fine 28 Days.

And then we have Limp Bizkit and here we have a problem because while acts like The Bloodhound Gang and Blink 182 have revelled in the sophomoric excess of the Beasties' early work, Fred Durst and Co., though clearly aware of *Licensed To Ill*, have incorporated none of the LP's spirit of fun into their music. There's no nudge-nudge, wink-wink on records like *Chocolate Starfish & The Hotdog Flavored Water*, just barely suppressed rage. Durst has simply stolen the Beasties' Zeitgeist. No wonder you can now buy T-shirts bearing the slogan 'Limp Bizkit Is A Crime.'

Collaborators & Cohorts: If showing the Beasties the way forward wasn't enough, Run DMC also contributed lyrics to *Licensed To Ill*. 'Slow And Low' was, in fact, scheduled to appear on *Raising Hell* but Joe Simmons fell out of love with the song. Discovering the track on a tape he liberated from Russell Simmons' desk draw, Mike D asked whether it would be cool if the boys worked over the track and after a few minor rewrites (lines like 'We're Run DMC not Cheech and Chong' had to be altered for obvious reason), 'Slow And Low' had become Beastie property. Simmons and McDaniels also had a hand in writing the odd but highly enjoyable 'Paul Revere.'

Beastiality: For an LP that is vastly different to the rest of their output, *Licensed To Ill* still features much that is recognisably Beastie. Sure, there are more references to guns and violence than there are on the rest of the boys' albums put together but the obsession with food and drink is familiar (Brass Monkey, an alcoholic beverage mildly less dangerous than meths, and White Castle, the American equivalent of the sit-down Wimpy joints of the 1980s, crop up seemingly every other line) as are the group's preoccupations with name calling (MCA gets a tough time from the boys because of his choice of sleeping companions) and getting in your face (between 'Slow & Low' and *Check Your Head*'s 'Pass The Mic,' the boys' position on this issue would not change one iota). There's also a smattering of pop culture posturing with Charlie Chan, Jerry Lewis and *Columbo* all receiving name checks. A few motifs are also set in stone with Adrock's obsession with his birth date and spelling out his name and the Beasties' desire 'to get nice' (which they were still talking up on *Hello Nasty*) all getting their first airing.

The Samples: Besides the Bonham loops on 'Rhymin' & Stealin',' which are taken from 'When The Levee Breaks' on *Led Zeppelin IV* or *The Four Symbols* or whatever it's called, and a snatch of the Clash's version of 'I Fought The Law' on the same track, there are a whole bunch of guitar riffs that, although not fully identifiable, sound as though they could have been lifted from White Snake and/or Motorhead records. Of course, it's possible that they were generated fresh in the studio. Otherwise there are odd bits and pieces to be found here and there, including a snippet from the *Mister Ed* theme tune on 'Time To Get Ill.' However, as Angus Batey explains, *Licensed To Ill* is a pretty basic album musically so there is none of the frantic cut-up work that would characterise the boys' later releases.

The Miscellany: Licensed To Ill (working title: *Don't Be A Faggot*) is dedicated to Adrock's late mother Doris Keefe Horovitz.

As the band proudly boasts on their Website, the record has become something of a mainstay on the US album chart. To this day, it continues to sell over 10,000 copies a week putting it in the same long stayer league as Pink Floyd's *Dark Side Of The Moon*, Bob Marley's *Legend* and, ahem, Jimmy Buffet's *Songs You Know By Heart*.

Regarding the titling of some of the tracks, 'Fight For Your Right' was released as a single in the UK as '(You Gotta) Fight For Your Right (To Party).' Likewise, 'The New Style' was originally released in the US as 'It's The New Style.' 'Rhymin' & Stealin'' is often listed as 'Rhyming & Stealing' or 'Rhymin' and Stealin'.' It's also important to note that different singles were released on either side of the Atlantic. 'Hold It Now, Hit It' and a double A-side of 'Paul Revere'/'It's The New Style' were put out on 12 inch in the US but not the UK. There, glad we got that straightened out.

The Verdict: With each passing year, the Beastie Boys seem to become more and more embarrassed about *Licensed To Ill*. Adam Yauch has developed such a loathing for the album that an entire page of the booklet that accompanies the *Anthology* compilation is given over to apologising for what the boys were and to trying to justify the inclusion of 'Fight For Your Right' on the retrospective. Personally, I don't think the boys have anything to reproach themselves for. While I don't buy the argument that the record is a full-blown parody (Adrock is now quite up front about the fact that while he's not homophobic anymore he was at the time he made *Licensed To Ill*), you only need to look at Mike D's loo chain-and-VW-badge combination and examine the true extent of the album's violent content which basically consists of getting kicked out of burger joints to realise that the group was yanking the rap world's chain to a certain degree.

But even if *Licensed To Ill* was really the way the boys were, so what? They were young, successful, sexed-up guys with a hit sound. They were meant to behave like assholes. They're rock stars, for Christ's sake! Of course, it would be a different matter if they were still behaving like dickwads but the Beastie Boys realise that you can only behave like Aerosmith for so long. Even when they were fighting for their right to party, the group was subtly suggesting hedonism might not be the be all and end all of existence. Indeed, what makes *Licensed To Ill* extraordinary is its ability to make being young and dumb seem immense fun while also suggesting that there might be more to life than dogging birds, drinking and smoking buds. 4/5

The New Style

The first rap LP to top the Billboard album chart, *Licensed To Ill* shifted over 5 million units. But were the Beastie Boys happy? No they weren't. They might have been chuffed that they'd never have to worry about money again but the experience of touring the album (see Alive) had left the boys jaded and uncertain of their true popularity. The group was also far from impressed with Rubin's recording strategy that basically centred upon making *Licensed To Ill II*. Throw in the fact that the Beasties believed Simmons was withholding money from them and you begin to understand why the band was so determined to distance themselves from the men who had made them millionaires many times over.

Disenchanted, the Beastie Boys went on hiatus for almost three years. They would not return until they discovered a new sound. A very new sound, indeed...

Paul's Boutique (1989, Capitol Records)

Catalogue Number: EST 2102

Producers: The Beastie Boys, The Dust Brothers and Mario G Caldato Junior

Track Listing: 'To All The Girls...,' 'Shake Your Rump,' 'Johnny Ryall,' 'Egg Man,' 'High Plains Drifter,' 'The Sounds Of Science,' '3-Minute Rule,' 'Hey Ladies,' '5 Piece Chicken Dinner,' 'Looking Down The Barrel Of A Gun,' 'Car Thief,' 'What Comes Around,' 'Shadrach,' 'Ask For Janice,' 'B-Boy Bouillabaisse' – (a) '59 Chrystie Street,' (b) 'Get On The Mic,' (c) 'Stop That Train,' (d) 'Year And A Day,' (e) 'Hello Brooklyn,' (f) 'Dropping Names,' (g) 'Lay It On Me,' (h) 'Mike On The Mic,' (I) 'AWOL'

The Japanese Version also features: '33% God' and 'Dis Yourself in '89 (Just Do It)'

In Brief: The boys ditch the style that made them millionaires and set about completely reinventing hip hop. A puzzled record-buying public stays away. A pissed-off record company starts asking awkward questions...

The Origins: Paul's Boutique might have been a very different album had it not been for the Beastie Boys' party-going habits. At a shindig in Los

Angeles in late 1988, the group found themselves listening to an extraordinary sound that Adrock would later describe as "four break beat records being played over one another." The instrumentals were the handiwork of Matt Dike, John King and Mike Simpson, alias The Dust Brothers. The collective had already tasted some success working with Tone Loc, he of 'Funky Cold Medina' and 'Wild Thing' fame. Indeed, the music the Beasties heard that evening were the backing tracks for Loc and Young MC records. It was enough, however, to sell Yauch, Horovitz and Diamond on the idea of recording their next LP with the Brothers Dust. Free from Def Jam, the band signed to Capitol for a massive undisclosed sum, quit New York and relocated to LA where they were put up in a rented mansion that would become known as the G-Spot. Much heady behaviour ensued...

The Standout Track: 'Shadrach.' The album in miniature, 'Shadrach' is rich in Sugar Hill Gang samples, pop culture references (the very first line is a direct lift from the *Batman* of the Adam West era), stoopid rhymes and fruity loops. If you can have a better time in four minutes and 14 seconds, I want to know about it. As for the title and the chorus refrain ('Shadrach Mesach Abednago'), it refers to three Biblical characters that were condemned by God to live in a fiery hole which they took to with the same relish that Charlie Sheen took to cocaine.

The Prime Rhyme: Paul's Boutique is dripping in rhymes that straddle the fine line between clever and stupid. As celebrations of silliness go, you'll be hard pushed to find finer than 'Shake Your Rump': 'Got arrested at Mardi Gras for jumping on a float/My man MCA's got a beard like a billy goat.' And speaking of MCA, he effortlessly pulls off his favourite trick of taking the piss out of himself on 'The Sounds Of Science': 'People always ask what's the phenomenon/Yo, what's up? Know what's going on?/No one really knows what I'm talking about/Yeah, that's right, my name's Yauch.' But for the best mix of the daffy and the daft, look no further than the aforementioned 'Shadrach': 'Only 24 hours in a day/only 12 notes a man can play/music for all, not just one people/and now we're gonna bust on the *Putney Swope* sequel' – the genius bit here being that in giving props to Robert Downey Senior's film about a company that hires black workers to make it more hip, the boys prefigure the launch of their own Grand Royal, a firm that saw chaos as a necessary adjunct to creation.

The Cover: A superb, seemingly early morning 360-degree shot of Paul's Boutique and its surrounding neighbourhood. The sleeve is so cool, in fact, that when an anniversary edition of the LP was released, a special limited edition T-shirt bearing the cover was also commissioned.

Influenced By: As it was sculpted by The Dust Brothers, *Paul's Boutique* owes a huge debt to the classic soul of the 1960s, the P-funk of the 1970s and the early rap experiments of the 1980s. In fact, there are so many Wilson Pickett, Sugar Hill Gang and O'Jays samples, you assume someone just went out and bought one of those *Greatest Funk Albums In The World... Ever* compilations.

Influences On: If there is one individual whose career hinged upon the release of the album and the emergence of The Dust Brothers, it's Beck Hansen whose *Mellow Gold* and *Odelay* albums were worked over by King and Simpson and who blends funk and Latino and soul and C&W together in a way that must make Messrs Yauch, Horovitz and Diamond proud.

Collaborators & Cohorts: A combination of a classically trained musician with a love of funk (John King) and a soul freak (Matt Dike), The Dust Brothers brought more to *Paul's Boutique* than a unique sound. Their gifts have, in fact, continued to shape the way the Beastie Boys make music. To think of the Beasties recording without Mario Caldato Junior and/or Money Mark, both of whom were introduced to the boys by the Brothers Dust is like trying to imagine them taking to the stage without Adrock or MCA. Dike, King and Simpson also inspired the relaxed recording methods that the boys would later employ. No great fans of studios, The Dust Brothers instead converted their lounge into a recording facility – the idea being that a more laidback atmosphere would lead to a more convivial sound. It's an interesting theory and one that clearly works for the Brothers, even if it does sometimes throw the artist they work with. Beck has even described recording with Dike and King as being a bit like "making a record in IKEA."

As for The Dust Brothers, Matt Dike has since quit the operation leaving Simpson and King to enjoy immense commercial and critical success producing artists like Beck and recording the soundtrack for David Fincher's *Fight Club*. They have also worked with teeny boppers Hanson.

The Samples: Besides all the funk and soul stuff, *Paul's Boutique* features snatches of The Beatles, elements of the scores from *Jaws* and *Psycho* which were composed by John Williams and Bernard Hermann, respectively, the same 'stop that train' sample (lifted from Scotty's 'Draw Your Brakes' which appeared on the *The Harder They Come* soundtrack) that Vanilla Ice used on his debut LP and a burst of Country & Western at the end of 'Hey Ladies' that presumably paved the way for Mike D's later Deep South experimentation (see *Anthology: The Sounds Of Science*). The LP also kicks off with something that sounds suspiciously like the noise the characters make when they run off in Hanna-Barbera animations – a weird but wonderful touch that lends a definite cartoon feel to the proceedings. *Paul's Boutique* is, in fact, what one imagines a record by the kids from *South Park* might sound like if Sly Stone produced it.

Beastiality: Like all self-respecting young men, the Beastie Boys realise that few things in life are as important as women, food, drugs, sport and old films and hence *Paul's Boutique* is littered with references to all five. On the film front, 'High Plains Drifter' takes its name from one Clint Eastwood film, name checks another (*Dirty Harry*) and then, for reasons best known to the boys, mentions the long-forgotten Peter Fonda vehicle *Dirty Mary, Crazy Larry*. *Die Hard*, *Rambo* and *A Clockwork Orange* all crop up on 'Looking Down The Barrel of A Gun' while the 'Stop That Train' cut from 'B-Boy Bouillabaisse' even manages to fit Dr Hfuhruhurr from Steve Martin vehicle *The Man With Two Brains* into the rhyme frame. 'Hello Brooklyn,' on the other hand, spoofs the opening number from Gene Kelly musical *On The Town*. There are also a lot of TV shows mentioned over the course of the album. The references to everything from cult successes such as *Welcome Back Kotter* which was the launch pad for John Travolta, and *Happy Days* to appalling trash like the Scott Baio vehicle *Charles In Charge* suggest that while the boys' taste in music is excellent, their viewing habits leave a lot to be desired. And if you're wondering what 'Sam the butcher bringing Alice the meat' on 'Shake Your Rump' means, it's a thinly veiled reference to the assumed affair at the centre of that most wholesome of American TV institutions *The Brady Bunch*.

As for the other stuff, the group takes off their collective hat to baseball star Mookie Wilson, talk about fried chicken and beer like they were going out of style and whitter on and on about smoking pot. If the group toked as much as they talk about it, they must have consumed as much cheeba as Bob Marley and The Wailers the night before they went through customs.

Keep an eye out too for some very strange non-pop culture references ('Johnny Ryall' drops the name of former New York City Mayor Ed Koch while 'The Sounds Of Science' gives props to Spanish explorer Ponce de Leon!), the use of now quite dated rap techniques such as the human beat box and all kinds of antiquated MC vocab. But while there are some references to guns and violence on *Paul's Boutique* ('24 is my age and 22 is my gauge' roars MCA on 'Looking Down The Barrel Of A Gun'), the LP is a pacifist work compared to *Licensed To Ill*. And while there is talk of drive-bys, they only involve raw eggs being thrown at surly doormen. You see, while the Beasties love hip hop they hate some of its conventions. It's for this very reason that they're able to take the mickey out of themselves since by showing that they don't take themselves too seriously, they're able to suggest that the rap community shouldn't be too po-faced either.

As is their wont, the Beasties also find time to give shout-outs to their affiliates with journalist buddy and occasional lyricist Tom Cushman receiving a big high five on 'The Sounds Of Science.'

The Miscellany: As Angus Batey explains in *Rhyming And Stealing*, the shop bearing the Paul's Boutique sign on the cover isn't the actual Brooklyn clothing emporium. Indeed, the shop pictured isn't even in Brooklyn but in Lower Manhattan. So what happened? According to Batey, the actual shop closed down but the group, having already chosen the name and sampled the Paul's Boutique radio advert, decided to press on and find another location that they could pass off as the original.

Incidentally, the fantastic cover shot was the handiwork of Nathaniel Hornblower, aka Adam Yauch. As for who Ricky Powell is ('Car Thief' – 'Homeboy throw in the towel/Your girl got dicked by Ricky Powell'), he's the bloke who took the surreal submerged inner sleeve photograph. Also involved in the cover design was one Jeremy Shatten, like Mike D a former member of The Young Aborigines.

The Verdict: There are some records in the world that you don't like to think about living without. Singles like Joy Division's 'Love Will Tear Us Apart,' Radiohead's 'No Surprises' and The Beatles' 'Yesterday,' albums such as Nick Drake's *Pink Moon* or Bob Dylan's *Blood On The Tracks*: if they didn't exist, it would hardly be worth getting out of bed in the morning.

The records that acquire indispensable status are usually quite emotional efforts. To lump an out and out good time record like *Paul's Boutique* in with such fraught, wrought works almost seems like bad taste. But in giving record buyers a chance to experience a party simply by slipping on a CD, the Beastie Boys have gifted the world something every bit as impressive as Dylan's willingness to open his heart or Kurt Cobain's desire to show us his frailty.

Paul's Boutique simply suggests that you can't have too many good times. Not as important as homelessness and drug dependency I'll grant you, but then the record does also address those issues. The Beasties, it seems, believe that everybody has a right to enjoy his or herself. But while they're as big on carousing as Dean Martin, the group is aware that happiness can come about as readily from affecting change as chugging beer and so *Paul's Boutique* bigs up the virtues of getting pissed *and* getting proactive, all to a backing track that's as dazzling as it is delightful.

The groundbreaking music and the record's lyrical *joie de vivre* have earned *Paul's Boutique* a reputation as the *Sergeant Pepper's Lonely Hearts Club Band* of hip hop. But while the similarities are stark (the Beasties' album features a reprise, 'The Sounds Of Science' samples 'When I'm 64'), the boys' record doesn't take itself seriously enough for it to be properly compared with the Fab Four's (over-)celebrated album. It can't even be seen in the same light as *Revolver*, the Beatles' best album in this writer's opinion, for although *Revolver* is a more entertaining record than *Sergeant Pepper*, it has acquired a worthiness that makes it a far from fun listening experience. As journalist David Quantick remarked in *Select*: "there are people in the world who believe that the two greatest albums in the world are *Revolver* and The Beach Boys' *Pet Sounds* and they never listen to either of them. You can see them when they go to each other's dinner parties: 'Oh look, you've got *Revolver* and *Pet Sounds*. Great! Let's not listen to them.'" Coincidentally, *Rolling Stone* magazine described the Beasties' LP as 'The *Pet Sounds* of hip hop.' *Paul's Boutique*, however, is a record you want to listen to. A lot. And believe me this record sounds just as good in your lounge at 10am on a Wednesday morning as it does in a club at 10pm on a Friday night. Put bluntly, this shit fits. 5/5

Get It Together

When he was asked about the recording of *Paul's Boutique* by MTV, Mike Diamond had nothing but good things to say about the project: "It was a nice time of friendship and collaboration. Everyone was expecting us to do this one thing and instead of doing that thing we completely broke South and that was something we were really proud of." D was less impressed about what happened after the LP came out: "Everyone at the record company got fired! No one wanted to talk to us. We were like: 'hmm, that's interesting.'"

Paul's Boutique sold 800,000 copies in the US – an astonishing number of units for such an experimental album but small fry compared to *Licensed To Ill*'s 5 million plus sales. Capitol certainly wasn't too impressed but, since it decided to cut the album's promotional budget as a punishment for the huge sums of money the boys had spent recording the album, it couldn't complain too much about its failure to equal *Licensed*'s success.

Capitol were ready to write off the Beastie Boys. The company had spent so much cash trying to land the band and had received such a small return on their investment they were prepared to just let the boys do what they liked with the rest of their advance and then give them the Spanish archer (translation: El Bow). Conscious that they really had ridden the torpedo to the end of the tube recording *Paul's Boutique* spending as much money renting air hockey tables as securing studio time, the Beasties underwent a second period of reflection. With *Boutique* engineer Mario Caldato and the estimable Money Mark now very much a part of the set-up, the group decided to save cash and construct their own recording facility. The end product of this ambitious but financially very sensible idea was G-Son, a studio built by Mark Nishita on the site of an old ballroom. A huge, open plan affair with a recording suite that doubled as a basketball and skateboarding facility, G-Son provided the Beastie Boys with somewhere to make music whenever they wanted while also giving them a place from which to run extracurricular activities like Grand Royal. Now effectively Beastie Boys Inc., the group embarked on their second stab at world domination...

Check Your Head (1992, Grand Royal/Capitol Records)

Catalogue Number: EST 2171

Producers: The Beastie Boys and Mario G Caldato Junior

Track Listing: 'Jimmy James,' 'Funky Boss,' 'Pass The Mic,' 'Gratitude,' 'Lighten Up,' 'Finger Lickin' Good,' 'So What'cha Want,' 'The Biz vs The Nuge,' 'Time For Livin',' 'Something's Got To Give,' 'The Blue Nun,' 'Stand Together,' 'Pow!,' 'The Maestro,' 'Groove Holmes,' 'Live At PJ's,' 'Mark On The Bus,' 'Professor Booty,' 'In 3's,' 'Namaste'

The Japanese version also features: 'Dub The Mic (Instrumental),' 'Drunken Praying Mantis Style,' 'Pass The Mic (Pt. 2, Skills To Pay The Bills)' and 'Netty's Girl'

In Brief: The boys rediscover their instruments and get funky (stop that now!)

The Origins: Perhaps the only good thing about the Beasties' early hardcore dabbling was that it gave the boys rudimentary, and I mean *really* rudimentary, skills as instrumentalists. As smack talking MCs, the trio had little need for musicianship. But, as Adam Yauch explains, the recording of *Check Your Head*'s predecessor had made the boys enthusiastic about getting back to their roots: "While we were working on *Paul's Boutique*, we started listening to a lot of funk and jazz stuff, looking for samples. We were trying to find records to sample and just listening to that kind of playing gets you back into the playing frame of mind. So right around when we finished *Paul's Boutique*, we started jamming."

The Standout Track: 'Pass The Mic.' A hard call this because both 'Gratitude' and 'Jimmy James' are also quite brilliant. In fact, it's hard to find a duff track on the LP. Such is the overall quality of *Check Your Head*, even the hardcore tracks work well! But no other song possesses quite the same awesome power as 'Pass The Mic.' I'm not sure whether it's the lyrical content or the strange wind chime-like sound during the introduction, but the track almost feels like a call to prayer. This is no boring *Songs Of Praise*-style sermon, though, it's a pumping, utterly positive essay on the pressures of life, the perils of fame and the importance of being yourself, all set to a groove you'd have to be dead not to feel. Come out the other side and you feel like you've been through the best kind of work-out, only here's it's your head and not your heart that'll benefit.

The Prime Rhyme: One of the first things you notice about *Check Your Head* is that the lyrics are incredibly difficult to decipher. This stems from the LP being recorded using cheap ass Japanese Karaoke mics that Mario Caldato bought the boys as Christmas presents. Personally, the distortion has never bothered me. Not only does it sound quite cool but I've always felt personal interpretation of song lyrics was a pretty important part of music. Thankfully other people seem to think so too, hence the success of *Check Your Head* and the existence of the very amusing Kiss This Guy Website (http://www.kissthisguy.com/intro.html) which is dedicated to misheard lyrics and derives its name from an idiosyncratic take on the last line of the first verse of Jimi Hendrix's 'Purple Haze' (my personal favourite example is the bloke from Truth Or Consequences, New Mexico, who was convinced Gene Pitney was singing: 'I was only 24/ I was from Tulsa').

But what of *Check Your Head*'s lyrical content? For this writer, the Beastie Boys have never been more intelligent and insightful than on their third LP proper. This isn't to say *Check Your Head* is up its own arse. On the contrary, it's often a lot of fun. As MCA wails on 'Professor Booty': 'You should have never started something/That you couldn't finish/'Cause writin' rhymes to me/Is like Popeye to spinach.' And when it's serious, it's only because it wants to do that rarest of things – be life affirming ('I don't see things quite the same as I used to' admit the boys on 'Stand Together' before concluding 'As I live my life I've got just me to be true to/And when I find that I don't know about just what to do/I turn and look within to see what I should do'). And while there are weaker moments like the hippy-ish meanderings of 'Namaste,' they're offset by rhymes that inform and empower such as this from the glorious 'Gratitude': 'Good times gone but you feed it/Hate's grown strong you feel you need it/Just one thing do you know/What you think that the world owes you?/What's gonna set you free look inside and you'll see/When you've got so much to say it's called gratitude.' Of course, this isn't a straight rap but, for my money, it's as stirring a verse as the band has ever cooked up.

By the way, if you want to find out exactly what the boys are saying on *Check Your Head*, proceed directly to http://www.beastieboys.com/lyrics_index.html.

The Cover: A great, understated photo of the band squatting down in their skate gear with only their instruments for company, looking like buskers on a cold November morning. The inner sleeve's also pretty cool. It features a nice portrait of Yauch, Horovitz, Diamond and Money Mark recording at G-Son on one side and a brilliant collage on the other capturing memories of great friends and good times.

Collaborators & Cohorts: As befits a stripped-down Beastie Boys record, there aren't too many guest appearances on *Check Your Head*. There *is* a great percussion section and both Biz Markie and Ted Nugent do their thang, but for the most part it's just the boys plus Mario C and Money Mark. Nishita actually receives billing alongside Yauch, Horovitz and Diamond on the credit sheet. He doesn't receive similar acknowledgement on the boys' later releases although this probably has as much to do with the success of his solo career as anything. Nevertheless, as Billy Preston added a certain *je ne sais quoi* to The Beatles' sound circa *Abbey Road* and *Let It Be*, so Mark Ramos Nishita's board work effortlessly augments *Check Your Head*.

Ted Nugent's contribution can't go completely without mention, either. An old skool American rocker who you may remember for 'Cat Scratch Fever,' Nugent is so politically incorrect (he loathes Paul McCartney for his drug use, eats red meat whenever he can and is so fanatical about his hunting he is a leading supporter of the National Rifle Association) his appearance on a reconstructed Beastie Boys record is rather like finding a copy of the *Diary Of Anne Frank* with a foreword by Martin Boorman. Just as he is pretty upfront about being an asshole, Nugent is also prone to contradiction, even coming out in support of Magic Johnson when the basketball player tried to use his brush with HIV to promote Aids awareness. It's because of this and his superior playing that his collaboration with Biz Markie, while jaw-droopingly weird, works quite wonderfully.

The Samples: As the vocal track is often far from audible, it's quite hard to identify some of the samples on *Check Your Head* since they're stirred so expertly into the mix. Sample spotting is made harder still by the fact that the Beasties lift a lot of loops from their rehearsal tapes. *Check Your Head* was edited down from over 100 hours of recordings and features fragments from all sorts of aborted tracks and half-finished numbers. Strap on your ear goggles, though, and you'll find elements lifted from numbers by 1970s soul giants The Isley Brothers and weirdo 1960s rejects The Turtles whose 'Happy Together' provided a minor hit for soap star turned coke head Jason

Donovan. Look out too for a healthy snatch of Bob Dylan's 'Just Like Tom Thumb's Blues' on 'Finger Lickin' Good.' Incidentally, Jimmy Walker, whose catchphrase "Dynamite" crops up on 'Pass The Mic,' was a trailblazing, pre-Richard Pryor black stand-up who was a regular on the panel at Dean Martin's Las Vegas comedy roasts.

One artist you won't find on the album, however, is Jimi Hendrix. Keen to give props to their idol, the boys had originally looped beats from a Hendrix track called 'Happy Birthday' around which they had built album opener 'Jimmy James.' Sadly, when Sir James' estate got word of what had gone down, they threatened legal action, so forcing the Beasties to record their own inferior version of 'Happy Birthday' that they in turn sampled. In the end, Hendrix's people relented but by then the album had gone to press. The superior 'original' cut does appear on the 'Frozen Metal Head' EP and the *Anthology* compilation.

Influenced By: Check Your Head is as much a funk album as a hip hop record. This isn't your pristine, shining-like-a-sunbeam Philadelphia funk sound, however. It's so dirtied up, you feel you should take a soak after listening to it. As such, the LP owes a big debt to George Clinton's more extreme work and to unsung genre legends Johnny Hammond and Freddie Hubbard, both of whose work is freely sampled on *Check Your Head*. The album also features a punked-up cover of Sly & The Family Stone's 'Time For Livin'.' There are actually quite a few similarities between Sly Stone's set-up and the Beasties'. Besides the love of soul and funk, the two groups have equally loose, multiracial set-ups. You could also make something of the fact that Sly and Mike D are both big dog lovers, although while Diamond's beloved Rufus receives song name checks and even appeared in the video for 'Sure Shot,' he is a very different animal to Sly's blind inbred pit bull terrier Gun who one afternoon raped and killed Stone's pet baboon after the band leader covered the monkey's favourite hiding place, an oak tree, in Vaseline. Incidentally, 'Time For Livin'' is the track that The Charlatans and The Chemical Brothers' reworked for the *Help* LP. And speaking of The Chemical Brothers...

Influences On: Listen to the Beasties' 'Namaste' and then tune into the Chemicals' *Exit Planet Dust* and *Dig Your Own Hole* and you'll see that the Brothers are clearly big *Check Your Head* fans. So too, according to Angus Batey's book, are Oasis who listened to the LP non-stop while touring the

44

UK in the early 1990s. Other artists who were clearly listening to the Beasties include Mo Wax giant DJ Shadow, production wiz Dan The Automator (Gorillaz, Handsome Boy Modelling School) and Belfast DJ David Holmes. When Shadow started dropping slices of soap operas and radio arts in amongst his tracks, critics started calling him the Jimi Hendrix of the turntables, oblivious to the fact that the Beasties' had been doing exactly the same thing eons earlier (*Check Your Head*'s 'The Blue Nun' being a case in point). As for Holmes, while his Moog-oriented soundtracks for *Out Of Sight* and *Ocean's Eleven* are excellent, they pale next to Mark Nishita's keyboard licks on *Check Your Head*. Okay, so the LP does occasionally sound like a cross between a 1970s cop show theme and the score for a porn film but, rest assured, we're talking about a helluva police programme and a bloody good blue movie.

Beastiality: As it finds the Beastie Boys trying out all kinds of new shit, *Check Your Head* also features some of the boys' favourite things. So in between being positive, the boys find time to scratch old spots like rubbish rappers (Professor Booty – 'So many wack MCs/You get the TV bozack/Ain't even gonna call out your names/'Cause you're so wack'). There's also some ace piss-taking going down with Adam Yauch's greying thatch coming in for some stick on one of the Mike D-sung verses of 'Pass The Mic.' And it wouldn't be a Beastie Boys record without lazy line fillers ('M.I.K.E. to the D' rhymes Mr Diamond on 'Pass The Mic' just four verses after Adrock pulls exactly the same trick), recording facility shout-outs (they give thanks for G-Son on 'Professor Booty'), props to Colonel Sanders (the very excellent 'Finger Lickin' Good') and plenty of cultural references, the only difference here being that it's not movies that they mention but American TV institutions like *Popeye*, *Star Trek* and *The Frugal Gourmet*. The track 'The Maestro,' meanwhile, features the sampled answerphone message trick the boys would reuse on *Hello Nasty*'s 'Three MCs And One DJ.'

The Miscellany: Check Your Head is dedicated to Adrock's best friend Dave Scilken who died of non-prescription drug use.

The Verdict: 'People how ya doing?/There's a new day dawning!' bellow the boys on the opening line of the opening track of *Check Your Head* and they're not lying. To reinvent the wheel twice in the space of as many records should be impossible and yet *Check Your Head* finds the Beastie Boys transforming once more, this time from three MCs into a bona fide band. And as with *Paul's Boutique* it's not the fact they've experimented that wins your admiration, it's the record. It's wonderful. Really, it's so groovy, it's actually very hard to write about. But, please, take my word for it, while it might be a million miles away from *Paul's Boutique* musically, *Check Your Head* runs its predecessor neck and neck in the quality stakes. 5/5

Assisted by some great videos and the Beasties' first global tour for five years, *Check Your Head* went platinum in the US. It didn't sell so well in Britain but no worries, the group had recaptured the ground they'd lost following *Paul's Boutique.* With a hit record, a new management contract with Nirvana's handlers Gold Mountain and a successful publishing and recording empire the group were again in a position to do what they wanted whenever they liked. Rather than push the envelope a third time, the Beasties decided not to push it at all.

Ill Communication (1994, Grand Royal/Capitol Records)

Catalogue Number: EST 2290

Producers: The Beastie Boys and Mario G Caldato Junior

Track Listing: 'Sure Shot,' 'Tough Guy,' 'B-Boys Makin' With The Freak Freak,' 'Bobo On The Corner,' 'Root Down,' 'Sabotage,' 'Get It Together,' 'Sabrosa,' 'The Update,' 'Futterman's Rule,' 'Alright, Hear This,' 'Eugene's Lament,' 'Flute Loop,' 'Do It,' 'Ricky's Theme,' 'Heart Attack Man,' 'The Scoop,' 'Shambala,' 'Bodhisattva Vow,' 'Transitions'

The Japanese version also features: 'Dope Little Song,' 'Resolution Time,' 'Mullet Head' and 'The Vibes'

A promo version of *Ill Communication* also exists with all the swear words removed.

In Brief: The band, realising that *Check Your Head* was a watershed release, go out and make the same record again only less successfully.

The Origins: In one of my earlier Pocket Essentials, I talked about how film director Sam Peckinpah (the man behind ace revisionist Westerns like *The Wild Bunch* and *Pat Garrett And Billy The Kid*) sometimes took his foot off the pedal to make genre movies like the Steve McQueen vehicle *The Getaway*. Well, *Ill Communication* finds the Beastie Boys in *Getaway* mode, crafting a safe, none-too-taxing follow-up to a genre-redefining work.

As befits a fairly unremarkable album, there's little that's interesting to report about the recording of *Ill Communication* other than that the boys cut the album in a small New York studio rather than G-Son. The reason given for the relocation was that the band didn't want to be distracted by their other Grand Royal commitments. Leaving their natural, nay spiritual, home did little to enhance the Beastie Boys sound, however. The band might go on about how the recording of *Check Your Head* meant they didn't have to fart around so much on *Ill Communication* but listen to both LPs and you'll agree that the Beasties sounded better mid- rather than post-experiment.

The Standout Track: While I've got a lot of time for 'Root Down,' an amazing, ass-kickin' piece of hip hop improvised after the album had been put to bed, I'd have to give the nod to 'Get It Together.' Most of the time, the Beasties have steered clear of whatever happens to be hot in the world of hip hop. 'Get It Together,' however, finds the group flirting with the gangsta style that was so in vogue in the mid-1990s (they'd previously stuck their big toe in the murkier end of rap music on *Paul's Boutique* with 'Looking Down The Barrel Of A Gun'). This isn't the same gang-banging, Uzi-fixated world inhabited by Snoop Dogg and Dr Dre, of course. Indeed, if Yauch, Diamond and Horovitz's posturing were any milder you'd assume they were taking the piss. The decision to work with Q-Tip, lead rapper with A Tribe Called Quest, does little to make the boys seem more macho since, along with De La Soul, Monie Love and The Jungle Brothers, ATCQ were leading lights in the hippie-esque, anti-guns 'n' violence Native Voices movement. The thing with 'Get It Together,' however, isn't that it's trying to muscle in on Niggers With Attitude's territory, rather that it's trying to illustrate how you can adopt that style but continue to sing about your traditional subject matter. So, rather than stuff about drive-bys and bitch slapping, you have lines about Adrock's marriage to Ione Skye which he compares to the happy union at the centre of *Happy Days'* spin-off *Joanie Loves Chachi*, a reference to legendary porn star John Holmes and Mike D giving props to his favourite New York Knick ('I've got heart like John Starks'). Sure, you get the band atypically using the term nigger and swearing a lot more than usual but you only need to check out the stance on drugs ('Never ever ever smoking crack/never ever ever fucking wack.') to realise the only drive-bys these boys are going to make are to McDonald's to stack up on quarter pounders. Quite simply one of the finest slices of hip hop to emerge from the 1990s, the only sad thing about 'Get It Together' is that Q-Tip seemed to get the wrong end of the stick and has since become a more mainstream (read: boring, boastful, gangsta-obsessed) performer.

The Prime Rhyme: Again, there are many candidates. The autobiographical stuff on 'Root Down' is a particular delight as is the final refrain that gives props to Mario C (can you imagine how much love there was in the recording studio that day?). The honour must go, however, to MCA's by turns boastful and self-deprecating stylings on 'Sure Shot': 'Timing like a clock when I rock the hip hop/Top notch is my stock on the soap box/I got more rhymes than I've got grey hairs/And that's a lot because I've got my share.'

The Cover: A strange black and white picture of a fat bloke ordering fast food at a drive-in counter that he clearly doesn't need. Far more appealing is the inner sleeve art work which features shots of the boys in their New York recording studio and an incredible painting that represents man's mistreatment of the environment or, at least, that's what I figure it represents: you'll really have to check it out for yourself. It's very strange.

Influenced By: Ill Communication represents the one and only time that the Beastie Boys have been guilty of following themselves. Outside of the samples that are taken from their favourite jazz and funk sources, it's hard to relate this release to any record other than *Check Your Head*.

Influences On: Such is the similarity to *Check Your Head*, it's almost impossible to say whether groups have been influenced by one record or the other. However, it's a safe bet to say that the Chemical Brothers, DJ Shadow, David Holmes, Dan The Automator and the Fatboy Slim were fans of the record.

Collaborators & Cohorts: Money Mark again delivers the goods on *Ill Communication* as does percussionist Eric Bobo who receives the honour of having a track named after him ('Bobo On The Corner') as does band photographer Ricky Powell ('Ricky's Theme'). *Check Your Head* alumnus Biz Markie who according to the credits 'appears courtesy of his own darn self' also brings his considerable weight to the table. Throw in Q-Tip, Eugene Gore – the violinist at the heart of 'Eugene's Lament' – turntable wizard DJ Hurricane who rather impressively wrote the chorus for 'Sure Shot' over the phone at 4am, and the phalanx of session musicians depicted on the back cover and you can see that *Ill Communication* wasn't short on collaborators. Indeed, what we might have here is a case of too many cooks spoiling the bad boy bouillabaisse.

The Samples: The only really big names to crop up on *Ill Communication* in sampled form are James Brown whose trademark grunt is briefly heard on 'Get It Together' and Richard Pryor whose comedy stylings appear on 'Fruit Loop' albeit in decidedly postmodern fashion, his contribution being part of a longer sample lifted from The Blues Project track 'Fruit Thing.' Kurtis Blow, who had a couple of minor hits in the UK in the early 1980s, also appears in equally convoluted form.

For the most part, though, the works sampled are little-known pieces by little-known artists, guys like Jim Steiga (who cut the flute solo used so superbly on 'Sure Shot'), Jimmy Smith and John Klemer who probably aren't even the most famous people in their own bathrooms. By the time they came to record the album, the Beastie Boys had become connoisseurs of vinyl to the extent that their record buying had even begun to rival that of Dust Brother Matt Dike who once famously bought 15,000 albums at an auction. The use of such rare samples is *Ill Communication*'s one area of excellence, since the fact you haven't heard the loops before means they don't draw attention to themselves. Rather than wasting time trying to work out which classics the boys have cut up, you simply sit back and enjoy the groove.

Beastiality: Ill Communication features more sports references than you can shake a caber-sized stick at. 'Tough Guy,' which starts out by laying into Detroit Pistons' hard man Bill Laimbeer, is so thick in basketball speak only a true fan of the game could fully fathom it. The same goes for 'B-Boys Makin' With The Freak Freak,' a tribute to the majesty of the New York Knicks.

The LP's also thick with evidence of the boys' movie love. 'Sure Shot' alone salutes awesome crime flick *The Taking Of Pelham 123* and Hong Kong action director John Woo who was virtually unknown outside of his native land at the time the guys decided to give him a shout-out. Elsewhere, the guys bang on about the *Star Wars* saga ('Do It') and the formidable Jean-Claude Van Damme ('Mullet Head').

The boys also big up their musical heroes. While Dr John and Lee Dorsey (he of 'Working On A Chain Gang' fame) are name checked on 'Sure Shot,' the group mentions old skool heroes on 'Root Down' and jazz legends like Les McCann, Yusef Lateef and Archie Sheep on 'Alright Hear This.'

As for other examples of Bestiality, the 'moneymaking' refrain first used on *Licensed To Ill* resurfaces on 'Root Down,' Mario Caldato and DJ Hurricane frequently receive respect over the course of the album and, in a rare moment of spite, the boys find time to stick the knife into their old Def Jam boss (to wit 'B-Boys Makin´ With The Freak Freak': 'Got fat bass lines like Russell Simmons steals money'). This later stuff is cool since it's always been the Beasties' policy to use their songs to essay their lives and thank their friends. *Ill Communication*'s name checking, however, verges on wretched excess. I mean, was it necessary to mention the likes of mass murderer The Son Of Sam, Branch Dividian leader David Koresh and ultra-feminist rock band Huggy Bear? Sure, the odd doffing of the cap is fine as is the occasional piece of pop culture but *Ill Communication* is so rich in references, it resembles a bowl of cereal with too many corn flakes and not enough milk.

The Miscellany: Ill Communication's sleeve notes explain that the royalties from 'Alright Hear This,' 'Shambala' and 'Bodhisattva Vow' will be donated to Aborigine Organisation, Tibet House and the Office Of Tibet.

Ill Communication inspired two spin-off EPs, *Root Down* and *Tour Shot*, which feature all the remixes of 'Root Down' and 'Sure Shot' you'll ever need plus a few more besides.

The Verdict: Ill Communication might start out big but it gets small quickly. Perhaps the only Beastie Boys album that seems to have filler tracks (*Hello Nasty* arguably commits the same offence only not on the same scale), the record might have seemed better had it not been released on the back of a truly great LP. And it would probably have seemed better still if it wasn't so similar in style to *Check Your Head*. What with its distorted Karaoke mics and super-fuzz effects, the record is practically inviting you to call it a sequel. Nevertheless, it's impossible to completely piss on an album that features tunes like 'Sure Shot,' 'Root Down' and 'Get It Together.' And even though songs like 'Sabotage' don't make great demands on the group, it has to be said that even at their worst, the Beastie

Boys are a damn sight better than a lot of bands when they're at the top of their game. 3/5

Ill Communication might have disappointed diehard Beastie fans but it shifted an awesome number of units. And even if the record wasn't to your liking, it was hard not to find affection for one of the LP's by-products…

The In Sound From Way Out!
(1996, Grand Royal/Capitol Records)

Catalogue Number: EST 33590

Producers: Various Artists

Track Listing: 'Groove Holmes,' 'Sabrosa,' 'Namaste,' 'Pow!,' 'Son Of Neckbone,' 'In 3's,' 'Eugene's Lament,' 'Bobo On The Corner,' 'Shambala,' 'Lighten Up,' 'Ricky's Theme,' 'Transitions,' 'Drinkin' Wine'

The Japanese version of the album also features: 'Get It Together (Buck Wild Instrumental),' 'Get It Together (ABA Instrumental),' 'Sure Shot (European B-Boy Mix Instrumental),' 'Sure Shot (Large Professor Instrumental)'

In Brief: A collection of instrumental numbers, B-sides and asides from the boys' two previous albums, some of which have been slightly reworked.

The Beef: The In Sound From Way Out! was originally given away free to members of the Beastie Boys' French fan club. Since only 200 copies were produced, the record instantly became very collectible. Ever determined to make sure their fans don't get ripped off, the boys decided to give the LP an official, 'nice price' release.

With sleeve notes in Franglais (sample – 'Les Beasties Boys – le groupe bad boy Américain') and a cover that, as Angus Batey points out, resembles continental Moog LPs of the 1970s, *In Sound…* really couldn't be more idiosyncratic. As for those who say that it couldn't be more superfluous, I can only refer you to another trend that my fellow author picked up on in *Rhyming & Stealing*. Invented by and named after the estimable Terry Moog, the Moog synthesizer has always had its constituency. In the late 1990s, however, the Moog became incredibly hot, cropping up on tracks by French dance acts like Daft Punk and Cassius. It also features heavily on Gallic duo Air's hugely successful *Moon Safari* LP and is used on DJ

Shadow's astounding *Endtroducing* and a number of other Mo' Wax releases. Now, it would be ridiculous to say that this rediscovery of an old skool synthesizer was entirely inspired by the Beasties. But if you consider the extent of the band's influence and the ease with which they fitted esoteric tracks like 'Sabrosa' and 'Bobo On The Corner' around chart-friendly material like 'Get It Together' and 'Root Down' on *Ill Communication*, it's fair to say that they might have had something to do with reclaiming instrumental music from the clutches of James Last and Richard Clayderman.

The Verdict: I have a friend who thinks that *The In Sound From Way Out!* is one of the greatest albums he's ever heard. I also have a friend who's convinced that Pontefract Cakes are a Chinese invention. This being the case, it's probably best not to place too much credence in what my friends think. For me, *In Sound...* is a pretty weird but rather wonderful release. When I used to listen to the boys' albums, I'd often skip over *Check Your Head* and *Ill Communication*'s instrumentals. It wasn't that I didn't like them, they just lacked the kinetic appeal of, say, 'So What'cha Want' or 'Root Down.' Heard in isolation, however, it's obvious that these numbers are far from fillers. On the contrary, there are funk workouts here that any band would be delighted to put their name to. And in prefiguring the second coming of the Moog and the emergence of DJ Shadow's introspective style of hip hop, the Beastie Boys again proved themselves to be way ahead of the game. Of course, since this material was previously available, albeit sometimes in a slightly different form, *The In Sound From Way Out!* is something of a luxury item. There are stupider things to spend your money on, however. Pontefract Cake, anyone? 3/5

The Skills To Pay The Bills

The combined success of *Check Your Head* and *Ill Communication* brought the Beastie Boys wealth and fame on a scale they hadn't enjoyed since *Licensed To Ill*. The albums also brought the band time in which to create album number five. Mike D has always said: "If a thing's worth doing, it's worth doing slowly!" and so it was that the boys spent FOUR FUCKING YEARS laying down the beats for what would become *Hello Nasty*. The lads took so long, in fact, they were able to dust off an eight-track EP prior to the LP proper.

'Aglio E Olio' EP (1995, Grand Royal)

Catalogue Number: GR206 (CD CDGRO26)

Producers: The Beastie Boys

Track Listing: 'Brand New,' 'Deal With It,' 'Believe Me,' 'Nervous Assistant,' 'Square Wave In Unison,' 'You Caught A Bad One,' 'I Can't Think Straight,' 'I Want Some'

The Japanese version also features: 'Soba Violence'

The Australian version also features: 'Soba Violence' and 'Light My Fire'

In Brief: Brief is the operative word as the band plough through eight hardcore numbers in a little over eleven minutes. You wonder whether they bothered to put a call through to *The Guiness Book Of World Records*.

The Beef: Taking its name from the most common of pasta dishes, 'Aglio E Olio' is what happened when the Beasties Boys began recording their hardcore contributions for *Hello Nasty* only to find themselves with far too many tracks. Released as an EP, the record contains formidable numbers about, amongst other things, such daily occurrences as fights in Tokyo noodle bars ('Soba Violence'). "If you're into it," comments Mike D in the *Anthology* sleeve notes, "you can check it out. If you're not, fast forward." There's no question that the boys are into it, though. They even toured the record, travelling across America, Japan and Australia under the pseudonym of Quasar and frequently taking to the stage in fancy dress.

The Verdict: Once again the Beastie Boys have a stab at hardcore and once again we all wonder why. I've almost come to the conclusion that the band's attitude to hardcore is the equivalent of Quentin Tarantino's attitude towards acting. Before making it big with *Reservoir Dogs* and *Pulp Fiction*, the young QT dreamt of becoming a leading man so once he became recognised as a writer and director, he used his newfound power to secure roles in flicks like *From Dusk Till Dawn*, *Destiny Turns On The Radio* and *Sleep With Me*. Of course, Quentin Tarantino isn't a very good actor but his work in front of the camera seems to make him happy. And, likewise, the Beasties seem to get off on hardcore – even though they suck at it – as it gives them an opportunity to professionally pursue what was their first musical love. Whether or not this is really the case, at least the existence of the 'Aglio E Olio' EP means that *Hello Nasty* is hardcore-free and for that we should all be grateful. 1/5

And after the appetiser, the main course...

Hello Nasty (1998, Grand Royal/Capitol Records)

Producers: The Beastie Boys and Mario G Caldato Junior
Catalogue Number: EST 495723 2
Track Listing: 'Super Disco Break-in',' 'The Move,' 'Remote Control,' 'Song For The Man,' 'Just A Test,' 'Body Movin',' 'Intergalactic,' 'Sneakin' Out The Hospital,' 'Putting Shame In Your Game,' 'Flowin' Prose,' 'And Me,' 'Three MCs And One DJ,' 'Can't, Won't, Don't Stop,' 'Song For Junior,' 'I Don't Know,' 'The Negotiation Limerick File,' 'Electrify,' 'Picture This,' 'Unite,' 'Dedication,' 'Dr Lee, PhD,' 'Instant Death'
The Japanese version also features: 'Slow And Low (Mix Master Mike Remix Version)'
On the US version of *Hello Nasty*, 'Can't, Won't, Don't Stop' is known as 'The Grasshopper Unit (Keep Movin')'
A limited edition also exists containing a second CD featuring the tracks: 'Hail Sagan (Special K),' 'Body Movin' (Fatboy Slim Remix),' 'Intergalactic (Prisoners Of Technology Remix),' 'Peanut Butter & Jelly'
In Brief: The band takes on the entire musical world and wins. Sort of.
The Origins: Lengthy development periods can be troublesome for bands since they create a crushing weight of expectation. To their credit, the Beasties are aware of the problem and even refer to it on 'Putting Shame In

Your Game': 'You'll be, like, Hello Nasty, where've you been?/It's time you're brought the grimy beats out The Dungeon.' The Dungeon, incidentally, is one of the many New York studios in which the band worked on the album and is also name checked on 'The Move.' Other venues used for recording included, of all places, Sean Lennon's loft apartment.

Whereas the boys had written their contributions to the two previous albums in isolation, they penned *Hello Nasty* together which perhaps explains the songs' high goof-off content and the LP's vocal inventiveness. On previous efforts, the boys tended to take one verse each but on *Hello Nasty*, you sometimes get all three guys styling on the same line: a tough trick to pull off unless you're very familiar with the material, you're very good mates and you're very talented. Thank God the Beasties are all three.

The Standout Track: 'Intergalactic.' If there was a better single released in the 1990s, I missed it. When it came out, I used to listen to Radio One for hours just on the off chance of catching it. Anyone who is aware of Radio One and its general output will understand the level of commitment this represents.

Not atypically for the Beasties, the song was several years in the making, as Adam Horovitz explained in the *Anthology* sleeve notes: "'Intergalactic' started out in 1993. We had this beat off a Bo Diddley record called 'Another Dimension' and we made this song all space doo doo rhymes about (astronomer) Carl Sagan, Lieutenant Uhuru and dilithium crystals. It didn't make the cut for *Ill Communication*. When we were making *Hello Nasty*, we had this one spaced-out hip hop song that nobody really liked. One night after fucking around with this song I was hanging out with my brother Matthew and some friends and our friend Penelope said: 'Whatever happened to that 'Intergalactic' thing you made?' The next day we made this ending part for the spaced-out song with this big beat that I had, and I said 'Intergalactic' through Mike's new Vocorder. The ending part was way better than the whole song so we just scraped it and made 'Intergalactic.' And because of Penelope, a lot of help from the board game Boogle and dreams of being flown around in a robot's papoose, it came out kinda nice." Do you reckon Westlife have ever made a record in the same fashion?

The Prime Rhyme: There's tonnes of fun stuff here, particularly on 'Unite' which gives Adam Yauch an opportunity to voice global concerns while simultaneously dissing his basketball team for its recent poor form

('Would someone on the Knicks please drive the lane.'). 'Three MCs...,' on the other hand, features nonsense verse of the kind Lewis Carroll would have killed to write ('My name is Mike D and I'm the ladies' choice/I want to get next to you, like Rose Royce'). But while the start of the second verse of 'The Move' secures the kookiness award ('Dogs love me cause I'm crazy sniffable/I bet you never knew I got the ill peripheral'), first prize proper must go to MCA for his new man-style declaration of intent on 'Intergalactic': 'Got to keep it going, keep it going full steam/Too sweet to be sour too nice to be mean/On the tough guy style I'm not too keen/To try to change the world I will plot and scheme.'

The Cover: A pretty groovy shot of the boys packed tightly in a giant sardine can, a situation the band actually sings about on 'Body Movin'.' The inner sleeve, meanwhile, is covered in enough space technology, graphs and maths equations to make Stephen Hawking moist. Now there's a pretty thought.

The Samples: Hello Nasty is probably the only hip hop record to feature snatches of *The Firebird Suite* by Leopold Stokowski and Rachmaninov's *Prelude C# Minor* (they crop up on 'Electrify' and 'Intergalactic' respectively). The album also includes several loops from the Pair Extraordinaire's eponymous LP, while 'Body Movin'' features an extract from 'Oye Como Va' by Latin legend and Lisa Simpson's best mate Tito Puente. Run DMC also make an appearance courtesy of a cut from 'Sucker MCs (Krush Groove I)' that crops up on opening track 'Super Disco Breakin'.'

Collaborators & Cohorts: Hello Nasty again showcases the talents of the world's best carpenter cum keyboard player Money Mark Nishita. By the time it came to cut the record, Nishita was already a respected artist in his own right thanks to his album *Push The Button* but it's good to see him still hanging out with his old friends. He has subsequently recorded a second, not quite so good solo LP, *Change Is Coming*.

Likewise, it's nice that Cypress Hill's Eric Bobo still fits in the odd freelance job. I'm figuring the boys' relationship with Bobo is a bit like the A-Team's relationship with 'Howling Mad' Murdock. They bust him out of Cypress Hill whenever they need him, then make sure they get him back before DJ Muggs and the others have had a chance to notice. The brilliant Brooke Williams also appears, singing superbly on 'Picture This' and 'Song For The Man,' and if you check out the backing vocals you can hear Grand

56

Royal affiliates Miho from Cibo Mato and Jill Cunniff from Luscious Jackson.

Besides these old faces, *Hello Nasty* features great work from two men new to the Beastie universe. A member of the Invisibl Skratch Piklz, Mix Master Mike only got the gig with the boys after he demonstrated his world champion scratch talents on a series of answerphone messages he left with MCA. Remembers Adrock: "We had this idea of having Mix Master Mike come out and help us on a couple of tracks. We wanted to do like an old skool two turntables and an MC kind of thing so we wrote some rhymes real quick and basically did 'Three MCs and One DJ' live."

Lee 'Scratch' Perry, on the other hand is quite mad (in an interview with *Neon* magazine, he explained that he hadn't bought into modern technology because: "God is my computer") but completely marvellous on 'Dr Lee, PhD,' even if he does continuously refer to the band as 'The Beastly Boys.' "Did we refer to Lee Perry as 'Mr Perry' or 'Sir'?," said Adam Horovitz in an interview with *Neon* magazine. "A little mix of both. The recording with him was done in New York. We'd gotten him the tape the day before and he came down and had the lyrics written on the back of a poster!"

Influenced By: You'd assume that after over a decade on the block, the Beasties might have got to the stage where they'd stopped worrying about what other bands were doing. Thankfully, the boys' hugeness hasn't led to arrogance and they're still pursuing fresh beats with the dedication of hunt hounds. The influence of Mario G Caldato Junior, whose family comes from Brazil, has been particularly positive, accounting as it does for MCA trying his hand at bossa nova on 'I Don't Know' and for the referencing of Tito Puente. The sampling of relatively obscure old skool outfits like the Pair Extraordinaire also proves that the band are still spending a healthy amount of time scouring their record collections, as does the desire to give props to old skool heroes like Run DMC – a nice touch since it allows the boys to revisit their *Licensed To Ill* origins and so add some symmetry to their amazing musical voyage.

Influences On: Is it just coincidence that a short while after the Beastie Boys rediscovered the delights of goofing around again, you had The Bloodhound Gang singing about 'doing the sort of stuff that only Prince would sing about' on 'The Bad Touch,' Blink 182 streaking naked through their home town in their promo for 'What's My Age Again?' and every other band in America owning up to sophomoric behaviour? Possibly, but then again, possibly not.

Beastiality: Hello Nasty wears its beastiality like a badge of honour. All the group's preoccupations and idiosyncrasies are present here. Besides giving props to Mario C on both 'Three MCs...' and 'Intergalactic,' the boys employ the 'moneymaking' motif on 'Unite' and 'Super Disco Breakin'.' The chaps also chuck in lots of references to their favourite pieces of technology, the SP-12 and the 808 and name check favourite films like *In Like Flynt*, *The Pink Panther* and *2001 – A Space Odyssey* (on 'Can't, Won't, Don't Stop') and *The Terminator* (on 'Unite'). They also go big on the sci-fi tip. Indeed, if you had a quid for every genre reference on 'Intergalactic,' you could probably retire. What's really amazing, however, is that, over a decade on from *Licensed To Ill*, the Beastie Boys still have concerns with such old skool standards as sucker MCs ('The Negotiation Limerick File'), being ill ('Unite') and b-boys and b-girls ('The Move'). They even use a bit of human beat box at the tail end of 'Can't, Won't, Don't Stop.' At least a few changes have been wrung – on 'Unite,' it's Mike rather than Adam H who keeps banging on about his star sign, although then again he did the same thing on *Ill Communication*'s 'Get It Together' so I suppose it doesn't really count. But while the group haven't lost their self-deprecating edge (as Adrock bawls on 'Unite': 'I went inside the deli and my man's like 'what?'/ I write the songs that make the whole world suck'), they've become pretty smart at creating their own legend through name checking their own songs. The aforementioned 'Unite' mentions *Paul's Boutique*'s 'The Sounds Of Science' and 'Shake Your Rump' and, in a gloriously postmodern moment, even refers to a song from *Hello Nasty*, 'Intergalactic.' And speaking of 'Intergalactic,' it actually features a snatch of *Licensed To Ill*'s 'The New Style.' Now, sampling your own material, that's clever. Perhaps a little too clever...

The Verdict: To begin with, a bit of a whinge. There are, I believe, some pretty perfunctory numbers on *Hello Nasty*. Sure, 'Intergalactic' would be worth losing a leg to listen to, 'The Negotiation Limerick File' is a truly trailblazing track and both 'Unite' and 'Can't, Won't, Don't Stop' would sit well on any Beastie Boys record. But since hip hop is supposed to be the band's meat and drink, the presence of a couple of shoddy rap numbers is wholly indefensible. There are also some rather incongruous moments such as when Adam Horovitz talks about his enduring pot habit on 'Unite' only to then sing quite movingly about his mother's death two songs later. It's kind of like hanging out with the worst drunk in the world, maudlin one moment, manic the next.

These gripes aside, it has to be said that the non hip hop material is frequently outstanding. 'Song For The Man' assassinates sexists to the accompaniment of cool Latin beats. The other experiments also work excellently, with the boys' first stabs at reggae, bossa nova and balladeering being so good, you could be forgiven for thinking they've been dabbling in these genres for years. In accomplishing this feat, the group outstrip most bands who seem to believe that simply setting out in a new direction will satisfy their fans. With the Beasties, it's not the experimentation that astonishes, it's the results.

The band's inventiveness is so impressive, in fact, that not only does it compensate for the duff tracks but it also means that *Hello Nasty* rivals, if not quite equals, the majesty of *Paul's Boutique*. Quite how the band take their music any further is hard to say. After spending time with *Hello Nasty*, however, your mouth will be watering about which dimension they decide to visit next. 4/5

It might only be the Beastie Boys' third best album but that couldn't stop the whole world falling in love with *Hello Nasty*. It really was hard to find anyone who didn't have a good thing to say about the record. Web publication Sonicnet.com commented that: '*Hello Nasty* works so well mainly because the album's a soundtrack for a party that – though begun years ago – feels like it's never going to end.' Michael Bonner at *Uncut*, meanwhile, wrote: 'This is blisteringly exciting stuff. Faultless? Guess so.' The album even got a positive review from *The Sun*, one of the British tabloids that had hounded the band throughout the 1987 Raising Hell tour.

The critical and commercial triumph of *Hello Nasty* led to a general resurgence of interest in all things Beastie. In an effort to both sate this fresh appetite and to mark the fifteenth anniversary of their first recording for Def Jam, the Beastie Boys decided to point up just how far both they and we had come.

Anthology – The Sounds Of Science
(1999, Grand Royal/Capitol Records)

Producers: Various Artists

Track Listing: 'Beastie Boys,' 'Slow And Low,' 'Shake Your Rump,' 'Gratitude,' 'Skills To Pay The Bills,' 'Root Down,' 'Believe Me,' 'Sure Shot,' 'Body Movin' (Fatboy Slim Remix),' 'Boomin' Granny,' 'Fight For Your Right,' 'Country Mike's Theme,' 'Pass The Mic,' 'Something's Got To Give,' 'Bodhisattva's Vow,' 'Sabrosa,' 'Song For The Man,' 'Soba Violence,' 'Alive,' 'Jimmy James (Original Version),' 'Three MCs And One DJ (Live Video Version),' 'The Biz vs The Nuge,' 'Sabotage,' 'Shadrach,' 'Brass Monkey,' 'Time For Livin',' 'Dub The Mic,' 'Benny And The Jets,' 'The Negotiation Limerick File,' 'I Want Some,' 'She's On It,' 'Son Of Neckbone,' 'Get It Together,' 'Twenty Questions,' 'Remote Control,' 'Railroad Blues,' 'Live Wire,' 'So What'cha Want,' 'Netty's Girl,' 'Egg Raid On Mojo,' 'Hey Ladies,' 'Intergalactic'

In Brief: The Beastie Boys whisk us away on a non-chronological trip through time that takes in 42 tracks, umpteen different musical styles and more samples than there are people in China.

The Beef: Anthology: The Sounds Of Science is no mere stop gap intended to keep the punters happy until the Beastie Boys brew up some fresh beats. With its ace front cover (a Spike Jonze black and white photo of the band dressed up as old men) and brace of booklets (the first a brilliant collection of photographs and essays by the band about the recording of each track, the second a double-sided effort featuring a black and white rendering of the *Paul's Boutique* cover and a selection of the group's album and single sleeve work), you don't have to be too smart to see that the band were hoping to do something very special here. To further underline this point, the group also kicked in some choice remixes like the Fatboy Slim take on 'Body Movin'' and the live video version of 'Three MCs And One DJ' and some new and previously unreleased material.

Of the extra stuff, the highlight is surely 'Alive' which was released as a single to promote the album. Unlike, say, the Pet Shop Boys' 'Was It Worth It?' which was one of two dire new tracks included on their otherwise faultless 'best of,' *Discography*, 'Alive' isn't a throwaway moment, rather it manages to encapsulate the Beasties' entire oeuvre while also pointing towards the new directions in which the group's music might be heading. The track almost feels like a Beastie manifesto, expressing frustration at the way things are while suggesting methods in which the world could be improved. Those on the Beasties shit list include gay bashers and those who'd prefer to spend income tax on building bigger bombs instead of building better hospitals (the track is possibly the only hip hop number to feature the word 'homophobics'). 'Alive' also takes a swipe at Limp Bizkit and their ilk ('Goatee metal rap please say goodnight.'), reiterates MCA's attitude towards narcotics ('Don't smoke cheeba, can't stand crack.'), gives props to people as varied as Pablo Picasso, Pele, Afrika Bambaataa, Mix Master Mike and Muhammad Ali, makes reference to DC Comics characters and Mike D's C&W alter-ego Country Mike, and sees Adrock utilise his favourite trick of spelling out his name when he's nothing better to say. That the band manage to cover all this ground in a four-minute hip hop song is breathtaking and, I'm sure you'll agree, is proof positive that, when it comes to beats and rhymes, the Beastie Boys represent very good value for money. As for the minimalist sample over which the song is sung, it is derived from 'I'm Still #1' by Boogie Down Productions, the ace New York recording outfit that featured KRS-One, a rapper best known to the greater music community for providing the rant at the end of R.E.M.'s 'Radio Song.'

Speaking of Mike D's country cousin, *Anthology* also gives the world a chance to hear the fruits of what have become known as the 'Country Mike Sessions.' Explains Adam Yauch: "At some point after *Ill Communication*, Mike got hit in the head by a large foreign object and lost all of his memory. As it started coming back, he believed he was a country singer named Country Mike. The psychologists told us that if we didn't play along with Mike's fantasy, he could be in grave danger." In truth, the persona of Country Mike simply gave Diamond a chance to live out a fantasy, just as Adrock's acting (see Beastly Movies) and MCA's charity commitments (see Milarepa) gave them the opportunity to realise their dreams of Hollywood stardom and saving the world respectively. Not that this means you should have to listen to the products of what MCA describes as a "tragic period of time."

Do, however, listen out for Yauch's previously unavailable but utterly charming 'Twenty Questions.' Recorded around the same time as *Hello Nasty*'s 'I Don't Know,' it is another ambitious attempt to lick a very complicated musical genre, bossa nova. As Yauch admits: "I couldn't stop listening to Jorge Ben and Antonio Carlos Jobin. At some point of listening to Jobin, I decided I wanted to write and record a couple of bossa nova songs. I guess that's kind of like saying: 'I was watching Michael Jordan play basketball and I decided that I want to play for the Chicago Bulls.' Sure you do." But from the sweet existential lyrics ('Are we intrinsically separate beings/or could we possibly be part of the same thing?') to the way Yauch's surprisingly soft vocals sit next to those of Cibo Mato's Miho, there's nothing here to scoff at and an awful lot to like.

The Verdict: Compilations being what they are, there's always a chance that the track selection is going to provide some disappointments. There are certainly some notable absences on *Anthology: The Sounds Of Science*. Of the singles from *Licensed To Ill*, 'No Sleep Till Brooklyn,' 'Girls' and 'She's Crafty' are all missing and there's also no room for 'The Sounds Of Science' itself. As for what has been included, there are a few too many hardcore numbers and did we really need more than one song from Mike D's redneck alter ego? That said, *Anthology* was intended less as a greatest hits package than as an attempt to bottle the band's essence, and once you accept this, it really is hard to see how the album could be more successful. By including every incarnation, every style of music they've experimented with, every single indulgence (their cover of Elton John's 'Benny & The Jets' featuring Biz Markie has to be heard to be believed), the group reveal themselves to be as honest as they are talented. Other bands judiciously select the tracks for their retrospective releases. Blur even hired a focus group to guarantee that their 'best of' had as wide an appeal as possible. The Beasties, however, have simply chucked in both the wheat and the chaff but since the chaff is rarely completely unpalatable and is frequently quite entertaining and as the wheat is very often wonderful, you never feel cheated. Actually, you feel pretty chuffed that the band thinks enough of their fans not to try and fool them. If only all history was related this way, maybe we might actually learn something from it. 5/5

So What'cha Want?

An 'Exclusive Interview' With Adam Yauch

Despite being a writer, I haven't met a lot of celebrities. Okay, so I've met Alex Cox but I always have to explain to people who he is. He's the director of *Repo Man* and *Sid & Nancy* and the original presenter of *Moviedrome*, by the way.

On one occasion in the late spring of 1999, I met not just a famous person but a real hero of mine. The Beastie Boys were in Europe touring *Hello Nasty* and I, as a journalist and fan, was going to make sure I met at least some of them. And so it was that I set up camp into the lobby of a vaguely famous London hotel. Tracking stars down in London really is a doddle. If you ever hear about Madonna fans spending hours traipsing around the city trying to find out where their heroine is holed up, they clearly aren't that dedicated. A writer to a degree that I was still using the prefix 'aspiring,' it didn't take more than phone calls to my two industry contacts – both of whom specialised in film rather than music – to pinpoint the Beasties' whereabouts.

Finding the band had been simple, but whiling away hours in a hotel lobby without looking like a rent boy looked a much harder proposition. Fortunately for me it was only twenty-five minutes into my vigil/stakeout/ stalking (call it what you will), that a familiar face appeared. There striding across the lobby in his hooded jacket, sweat pants and trainers was MCA himself – Adam Yauch!

"Wow!"

Yes, I actually said "Wow!"

For a moment, I didn't know what to do. Then I leapt into action. Bounding up to him with the enthusiasm that a cocker spaniel bounds up to... well, anybody I suppose, I immediately engaged my idol in conversation.

"Hello, Mr Yauch! How are you enjoying London?" On the list of stupid things I've said, this is right up there with my going up to a 6' 8'' bloke on my first day at university and remarking: "You're very tall, aren't you?" MCA, however, was happy to indulge the oaf grinning before him.

"Hey, man. Yeah, it's great to be back." What a gent, I thought. He's let me off the hook. Everything will be OK now. All I have to do is not say something stupidly predictable like how much I like the new album.

"The new album's great!" I heard myself saying while simultaneously seeing myself lose whatever credibility I'd remembered to pack.

"Oh, I'm glad you like it," smiled Yauch, again fielding a question he must have been asked a thousand times with all the politeness of an Indian shopkeeper during a royal visit. I bet the MCA household is one where the Jehovah's Witnesses get asked in for tea and are offered the nice biscuits.

Before I could further jeopardise what passed for my reputation, a large black gentleman joined us. "Hey, MCA, the car's here."

Hey, MCA? A little informal, I thought. Surely, Mr Yauch would have been more appropriate. Or failing that, Mr MCA.

"Hey, man, gotta go," said Mr Yauch. "See ya round." Which I thought was nice since it presupposed that we will meet again someday. Admittedly, he hasn't called yet, but I figure it's only a matter of time.

And then he was off to create more mind-blowing music, to continue his one man war on China, to do battle with alien races or, as is perhaps more probable, to rehearse for that evening's performance at Wembley Arena. I, meanwhile, looked down at the bag containing my unsigned copies of *Hello Nasty, Check Your Head, Ill Communication, Licensed To Ill, Paul's Boutique, Some Old Bullshit* and *The In Sound From Way Out!* and smiled the way only a man who has had a fleeting encounter with his biggest hero can smile. In my heart of hearts, however, I felt the way a Christian might feel if he briefly encountered Jesus but only managed to blurt "so, when's the new book out?" during their time together.

Still it could have been worse. When I met Clint Eastwood, I got so excited I ended up stealing his water bottle. Oh yes, I have met Clint Eastwood! And you know what? He likes London, too!

Milarepa

The Beastie Boys Take On China And Try To Free Tibet

So you've sold truckloads of albums, reinvented hip hop, launched your own record label and publishing company and proven yourself to be amongst the world's finest music video makers. What do you do next? Go to war with China, obviously.

If Adam Horovitz is the Beasties' Mr Music and Mike Diamond is the band's businessman, then it is with some justification that Adam Yauch can claim to be the group's spiritual presence. A keen student of Buddhism since the early 1990s (it's not known whether he's fully converted to the faith), it's rather appropriate given the Beasties' early indulgent phase that Yauch should have his first serious encounter with the faith while enjoying something as hedonistic as a snowboarding holiday. Having conquered the slopes of Utah, MCA travelled to Nepal in 1990 to tackle the might of the Himalayas. Recalls the rapper: "I was reading a lot about Native American and other religions and checking out different things. Then I was in Kathmandu and I met some people who were Tibetan Studies majors. I was just hanging out with them; went to a couple of monasteries and Tibetan people's houses and started getting into Tibetan culture a little bit." Of the people he met, student Erin Potts was perhaps the most important in terms of explaining Buddhist beliefs to Yauch and informing him about the hardships Tibet had suffered since the invasion by the People's Republic Of China in 1955. Fascinated by what he had learned, MCA (who had exhibited existential leanings on the *Paul's Boutique* track 'A Year And A Day') resolved to learn more about Buddhism and the Tibetan cause.

Of course, for most backpackers, this further involvement would have consisted of lighting the occasional joss stick, buying a few George Harrison albums and briefly (and probably disastrously) experimenting with tantric sex. MCA, however, really went back to school, buying up important texts and attending seminars. As he explained to *Bomb* magazine: "It just seemed like Tibetan Buddhism was a real solid organisation of teachings to point someone in the right direction." Yauch's quest even resulted in an encounter with the great man himself His Holiness The Dalai Lama who, as Yauch recalls in the sleeve notes to *Anthology: The Sounds Of Science*, walked straight up to MCA and burst into laughter! It was such a disarming gesture that Yauch couldn't help but beam back.

Buddhism also began to have an impact upon the Beasties' music. Explains MCA: "In meditation, I work on visualisations of what the music represents or feels like to me and then when it comes time to write, it just pretty much just comes through." Besides Buddhism affecting Yauch's songwriting, *Ill Communication* actually contained two tracks, 'Shambala' and 'Bodhisattva Vow,' that featured sampled Buddhist chanting and elements of the faith's teachings. 'Bodhisattva Vow' is, in fact, a very ambitious attempt to compress the work of Shantideva, an Indian scholar from the eighth century, into a four-minute hip hop number. Neither song is wholly successful but they reveal that Yauch's interest in the faith is far from passing and that, in happily indulging their buddy, Diamond and Horovitz possess a very attractive altruistic streak.

Adrock and Mike D also backed MCA's efforts to make sure that the Buddhist monks they had sampled for the *Ill Communication* tracks received royalties. When he asked Erin Potts what the best way to repay the holy men might be, the student replied that it would be nice if MCA could help set up a fund to support Tibetan charitable causes. Being a Beastie Boy, Yauch did more than just kick a few bucks the way of Central Asia. In 1994, he and Potts established the Milarepa Fund, which in the words of its mission statement, is: 'a non-profit organisation that actively supports the Tibetan people in their struggle to regain independence.'

As enamoured as he was with Buddhism, MCA was also appalled by the near genocidal crimes that had been inflicted upon the Tibetan people. He was adamant however that, as his hero Dr Martin Luther King Junior had insisted, all protest should be of the non-violent variety. As he explained in the Milarepa mission statement: 'through non-violence, Tibet survives as a living example of compassion and the positive social principles required to affect meaningful change. It is because of this that we believe that helping Tibet will ultimately be of benefit to all humanity.'

So instead of taking up arms, Yauch suggested that people avoid buying products made in China (many of which are produced under appalling sweat shop conditions) and boycott US companies known to have close dealings with the Chinese government such as Pepsi, whose tasty beverage is distributed across China by the Red Army, aka the loveable rogues who orchestrated the slaughter of thousands of students in Tiananmen Square in 1989. MCA's worthy efforts were somewhat hamstrung when, in its infinite wisdom, the American government granted China, the country with the world's worst human rights record, favoured nation trading status.

This setback has not dented MCA's commitment to the cause. Indeed, the worse the circumstances get, the more determined he seems to make both Milarepa work and Tibetan freedom become a reality. He was even magnanimous enough to give props to China on the *Hello Nasty* cut 'Dedication' ('This goes out to Tonga, Beijing, The Dubai Brothers, Miami...') – this in spite of the fact that the Chinese government have banned the sale of all Beastie Boys records and merchandise and openly opposed their Tibetan Freedom Concerts. "To us that statement was a positive thing," Yauch told *Neon* magazine. "It just calls attention to the fact that if that's how the Chinese government is reacting to people's freedom of speech outside of the country, then you can only imagine how people inside the country are being treated. But I think you have to separate the people from the threats. It's still important to give people all over the world a shout-out."

By way of a digression and without wishing to make it sound too much like I want to blow him, Adam Yauch is actually a pretty remarkable young man. The dumb kid with a beard like a billy goat has grown up to prove that all that bullshit about how hard it is to be a man these days is just that: bullshit. There are, in fact, lots of blokes around these days showing that you can still be a real man and not be a real asshole at the same time. Johnny Depp, Henry Rollins, Huey from the Fun Lovin' Criminals – these are all men to look up to, people who have talent but who also have a grasp of humility and an understanding of self-deprecation, who can be sexy without being sexist and who realise that being young doesn't equate with being useless. And if these guys are the new princes of the universe, Adam Yauch is their king. A happily married, spiritually in touch with himself family man who has the skills to pay the bills and the desire to save the world, MCA is one of the best arguments the human cloning lobby has going for it – with a few more Adam Yauchs, the world really would be a better place.

And of his many spiritually oriented successes, arguably Yauch's greatest triumphs have been the Tibetan Freedom Concerts. Inaugurated in 1996, the first gig was held over a weekend in San Francisco and featured such choice acts as A Tribe Called Quest, Beck, Bjork, De La Soul, Foo Fighters, The Fugees, John Lee Hooker, Pavement, Rage Against The Machine, Red Hot Chili Peppers, The Smashing Pumpkins and Sonic Youth. Since it raised over $3m for Milarepa, you won't be surprised to hear that the concerts have become something of a staple on the US festival circuit. There's more to the gigs than just fundraising, however. Besides raising awareness about Tibet and its ongoing struggle, Yauch has also provided America's so-called slacker youth with an opportunity to show that it cares. You only need to look at the T-shirt sales to see that it does. And you only need to look at Adam Yauch to see that, while one man might not be able to beat a nation of billions, he can certainly point up its failings and aid those it oppresses. Like they say in Australia: you're a legend, Adam Yauch.

> 'I wish for peace between the races/
> someday we shall all be one'
>
> > 'Something's Got To Give,' Check Your Head

For more information about the Milarepa Fund, please visit its US Website at -http://www.milarepa.org/ or its Japanese affiliate at − http://www.milarepa.org/japan/ They're both fantastic sites. The American wing in particular makes the fund's goals clear but also manages to mix up its serious message with fun stuff like film, album and theatre reviews and even recipes. News about Milarepa activities and Tibetan Freedom merchandise can be found at the Beastie Boys official site (http://www.beastie-boys.com/).

Video Vanguard

Even if their music hadn't been up to much, it's still possible that the Beastie Boys would have found a place in pop's pantheon thanks to their visual flair.

Fresh out of the blocks, the Beasties had a keen understanding of the promo video. This isn't too surprising if you consider that Yauch, Horovitz and Diamond belonged to the first generation raised on music television. By 1986, MTV had been broadcasting for the best part of five years and legendary clips had already been created by A-ha ('Take On Me'), Dire Straits ('Money For Nothing') and Madonna (take your pick). Interestingly, the influence on the boys' early work came not from the slickness of, say, Russell Mulcahy who was behind Duran Duran's exotic 'Rio' and 'Hungry Like The Wolf' clips but from the tongue-in-cheek, Benny Hill-style comedy of former Van Halen front man David Lee Roth. When MTV aired the Beasties' videos for 'She's On It' (cue: the boys walking up and down Long Island beach, ogling a bikini-clad woman and completely failing to get off with her) and 'Fight For Your Right' (cue: the boys holding a party at a mate's house, gobbing beer over people, groping girls and chucking custard pies), people were up in arms. Look at the clips now, though, and they're no more upsetting than Lee Roth's reworking of 'California Girls.' Calculating and a little crass they might be but the Beasties' first vids were sexy rather than sexist. And, of course, what's wrong with being sexy?

Although they kept up their cheeky monkey act up for all the *Licensed To Ill* single releases, by the time *Paul's Boutique* came out, the group's visual style had changed utterly. The biggest advance was that instead of hiring directors, the group or rather Adam Yauch under the guise of his led-erhosen-sporting, Swiss-born alter ego Nathaniel Hornblower, had taken the helm. Opening his account with the clever, animated video for flop single 'Shadrach,' Yauch soon evolved the Beasties' trademark style. MCA's technique was incredibly simple: just stick a camera on the ground (fish eye lens optional) and let the boys rap directly into it. It couldn't have been more straightforward but since it brilliantly reflected the boys' in-your-face style, it's hard to see how it could have been more effective. First experimented with on the promo for 'Shake Your Rump,' Yauch had the style nailed down with spikes by the time he came round to shooting the land-

69

mark videos for 'Pass The Mic' and 'So What'cha Want' (on the latter, the technique was further augmented by the use of slow mo and some rather impressive jumping). Further fresh touches were employed on the clip for 'Sure Shot,' a retrospective favourite on VH-1 throughout 2001, that featured the standard low camera as well as a camera hung from a crane and footage of the boys sporting tuxedos and throwing martial arts shapes while on a night on the lash in Las Vegas.

As good as MCA's work on 'Sure Shot' was, it was the non-Yauch directed video for another track from *Ill Communication* that was to set the seal on the band's reputation as masters of short form film-making. Now best known as the genius behind the idiosyncratic, idea-heavy *Being John Malkovich*, Spike Jonze (born Adam Spiegel in 1969 in Rockville, Maryland) enjoyed his first dose of fame making music videos. The director of the clips for R.E.M.'s 'Electrolite' and 'Crush With Eyeliner,' Bjork's 'It's Oh So Quiet,' Weezer's 'Buddy Holly' and 'Island In The Sun' and the award-winning Fatboy Slim videos for 'Praise You' and 'Weapon Of Choice,' Jonze came to promo making courtesy of the Beasties who'd tapped into his visual flair while Spike was editing *Grand Royal* magazine. Let loose on the band's 'Sabotage,' Jonze dreamt up a spoof cop show that was simultaneously a glorious homage to 1970s *Starsky & Hutch*-style television and the funniest short movie this side of Peter Sellers and Richard Lester's *Running, Jumping & Standing Still Film*. (Incidentally, it fell to Adam Yauch to explain the rigours of the 'Sabotage' shoot to MTV which he did with tongue firmly in cheek: "We were going undercover dressed as undercover cops and we started hanging out at the police station and we started to get a vibe for what being really deep undercover was really like.") With its use of stock footage and well-observed genre set pieces (ever noticed how whenever a cop tackles a con in an American TV series, there always happens to be a bunch of cardboard boxes or bin bags conveniently close at hand to cushion his fall?), the clip was so breathtaking it completely covered up the fact that the single was one of the band's weaker releases. And even if Jonze's visual flair wasn't to your liking, it was hard not to be amused by a cast list which featured such notables as Nathan Wind as Cochese, Sir Stewart St James as Himself and, lest we forget, Fred Ward as Bunny.

The award-winning clip for 'Sabotage' opened new doors for the Beasties. For so long the lords of lo-fi promo production, subsequent releases have seen the boys spoof such big-budget subgenres as the Bond movies (the video for 'Body Movin'' featured Adrock as a secret agent out to retrieve a chocolate sauce recipe from MCA's criminal mastermind and his bizarre, wig-wearing henchman played by Mike D) and the Godzilla series ('Intergalactic's clip pitted a colossal robot, piloted by the band, against a giant cockroach-like creation). The group hasn't completely turned their back on their old skool, in-your-face approach. Indeed, the videos for both 'Intergalactic' and 'Alive' feature substantial portions of straight-to-camera footage. And as they proved with their live clip for 'Three MCs And One DJ,' the Beastie Boys are still capable of spinning gold from the basest of elements. Three MCs, three cameras, one DJ, one take: it sounds like a recipe for disaster but when the boys are on top form, it's all they need to create video magic.

Beastly Movies

Conquerors of the small screen, the Beastie Boys have enjoyed considerably less success in the field of feature-length motion pictures.

Having proven that it was possible for rap music to enjoy mainstream success in America, Def Jam's Russell Simmons was keen to see if hip hop could thrive in other mediums. Some of these side ventures such as cable TV show *Def Comedy Jam* would prove big hits. Simmons' attempts to create rap movies, however, would result in two of the worst films ever made. Unfortunately, the Beastie Boys, as one of Def Jam's hottest acts at the time, were dragged into both fiascos. Not that the naïve, easily excited trio needed a lot of dragging.

Krush Groove (1985)

Cast: Sheila E (Herself), Joseph Simmons (Run), Darryl McDaniels (DMC), Jason Mizell (Jam Master Jay), Mark Morales, Damon Wimbley and Darren Robinson (The Fat Boys), Kurtis Blow (Himself), Blair Underwood (Russell Walker), Ricky Bell, Michael Lamone Bivins, Bobby Brown, Ronald De Voe and Ralph Tresvant (New Edition), Adam Horovitz, Mike D and Adam Yauch (Beastie Boys), Russell Simmons (Crocket), Rick Rubin (Rick)

Crew: Director Michael Schultz, Writer Ralph Farquhar, Producers Doug McHenry, Michael Schultz, Cinematographer Ernest R Dickerson, Editors Jerry Bixman, Conrad M Gonzalvez, Alan Kozlowski

The Verdict: The story of Simmons' rise to power could have made for quite an interesting biopic. This fictionalised account, however, is less rags to riches as dealers 'n' bitches. Blair Underwood plays Russell Walker, a daring young music exec who uses drug money to get his records pressed and who spends the rest of his time in competition with his brother (played, rather confusingly by Simmons' real-life sibling Joseph) for the affections of Prince's drummer Sheila E.

A distressingly bad example of what happens when people with money but no sense are allowed to run amok in the world of film, one of the movie's few saving graces is that it provides the basis for one of the funnier exchanges in Kevin Smith's religious comedy *Dogma*. Avenging angels

Bartleby (Ben Affleck) and Loki (Matt Damon) are crossing America via coach when their boredom turns to bickering. "This from the guy who still owes me ten dollars from a bet over which was going to be the bigger movie, *E.T.* or *Krush Groove*." "Hey, fuck you man," his partner replies, "time's going to tell on that one!"

And what's the other good thing about *Krush Groove*? The Beasties were able to restrict their participation to the briefest of cameos ("We're the band!" explains MCA to Run DMC before having a record broken over his head). 1/5

Krush Groove was an unmitigated disaster. So it was no surprise at all that, three years later, the people responsible decided to have a second bash.

Tougher Than Leather (1988)

Cast: Joseph Simmons, (Run), Darryl McDaniels (DMC), Jason Mizell (Jam Master Jay), Adam Yauch (MCA), Mike Diamond (Mike D), Adam Horovitz (Adrock), Rick Menello (Arthur Ratnor), Rick Rubin (Vic), Mickey Rubin (Marty), Russell Simmons (Himself)

Crew: Director Rick Rubin, Writers Rick Rubin, Rick Menello, Producer Vincent Giordano, Cinematographer Feliks Parnell, Editor Steven Brown

The Verdict: They really must have been smoking the chronic at Def Jam in the late 1980s. Rick Rubin must have been a particularly heavy user because he somehow managed to convince himself that his success as a record producer meant he was capable of writing and directing a feature film.

For the two of you out there that are interested, the movie stars Run DMC as themselves and centres on their quest to take down the drug lord who murdered their best friend. Perhaps best described as a cross between a blaxploitation movie and a Spaghetti Western, the picture has amazingly been ignored by serious film publications. The only time anyone connected with Def Jam has talked about the picture was when the late, lamented *Neon* approached Darryl McDaniels for an article about the nightmares that can occur 'When Rock Stars Act!' Asked about his work on the movie, the only positive things DMC had to say concerned working with the Beastie Boys – "They were great, just really, really nuts. We went to lunch together one

73

time and they gave all the waitresses the run around. They were the funniest guys." What's funny off screen isn't necessarily funny in front of the cameras, however. As it is, the boys couldn't look more out of depth if they were Toulouse-Lautrec taking a dip in the middle of the Pacific Ocean.

That *Tougher Than Leather* is actually worse than *Krush Groove* is a little like discovering that there really is a fate worse than death. It's so bad that it receives 2.2 stars out of 10 on the Internet Movie Database, placing it on the outskirts of the list of the worst 250 pictures on the survey. Put another way, if you find *Tougher Than Leather* at your local video store, never feel tempted to rent it – even if the only other things on offer are *Plan 9 From Outer Space*, the Richard Burton and Sophia Loren TV version of *Brief Encounter* and *Breakin' 2 – Electric Boogaloo*. 1/5

While the band's efforts to make it in the movies were epic failures, Adam Horovitz briefly threatened to become a genuinely interesting leading man. His films were mostly awful (you should steer well clear of *Roadside Prophets* and the meandering *Cityscrapes: Los Angeles* which he made with wife Ione Skye. And while you're about it, don't feel under any pressure to check out Mike D's pre-Beasties stab at acting in *Over Exposed*) but he did manage a passable cameo in James Dearden's remake of *A Kiss Before Dying* and on oné occasion at least delivered a truly compelling performance.

Lost Angels (1989)

Cast: Donald Sutherland (Dr Charles Loftis), Adam Horovitz (Tim Doolan), Amy Locane (Cheryl Anderson), Don Bloomfield (Andy Doolan), Celia Watson (Felicia Marks), Graham Beckel (Richard Doolan), Patricia Richardson (Mrs Anderson)

Crew: Director Hugh Hudson, Writer Michael Weller, Producers Thomas Baer, Howard Rosenman, Cinematographer Juan Ruiz Anchia, Editor David Gladwell, Music Philippe Sarde

The Verdict: The story of a youth raised around drugs, divorce and inner city crime and the psychiatrist who sets out to save him, *Lost Angels* exposed Adrock to a world he'd previously only read, written and sung about. Not that this lack of practical knowledge hampers Horovitz at all.

74

Indeed, he is so naturalistic and sympathetic that you really wish he'd pushed the acting a little further. Of course, it does help that he is working with the ever excellent Donald Sutherland and director Hugh Hudson who shot to fame in the early 1980s with a little something called *Chariots Of Fire*. Had he been working with Kiefer Sutherland and Gary '*Road House*' Hudson, the results might have been very different.

Yes, there are better films around and better performances but *Lost Angels* does stand apart from the John Hughes *rites du passage* movies of the same era and Adam Horovitz' work really does deserve a place in the 'great screen performances by rock stars' file alongside Mick Jagger's performance as Turner in *Performance*, David Bowie's turn as Mr Newton in *The Man Who Fell To Earth* and, er..., that's it. Film – 3/5 Horovitz – 4/5

If their dalliances with fiction film have been largely flawed, the Beasties' sole contribution to documentary cinema is genuinely impressive.

Free Tibet (1998)

Cast: Beck, Bjork, Smashing Pumpkins, Beastie Boys, Rage Against The Machine, Foo Fighters, Red Hot Chilli Peppers, De La Soul, A Tribe Called Quest, Sonic Youth

Crew: Director Sarah Pirozek, Producers Adam Yauch, Maria Ma, John Sloss, Laura Poitras, Christopher Covert, Jay Faires, Cinematographers Lance Acord, Morgan Barnard, Even Barnard, Roman Coppola, Tashi Dhondhup, Jonathan Hoare, Jarid Johnson, Spike Jonze, Kurt Wolf Langer, Tom Piozet, Ricky Powell, Editors Paula Heredia, Robert Nassau

The Verdict: A brilliant attempt to capture one of the more important concerts of the 1990s, it's hard to think of a major alternative act that isn't already on the bill. And if some of the discussion of Tibetan issues becomes a little repetitive, there's no doubt that those speaking have their hearts in the right places and at least they're never as trite as R.E.M.'s Michael Stipe who told BBC TV's *The O-Zone* that the reason he was supporting Tibetan freedom was because "orange is a really cool colour."

Interviewed by *Neon* about why he had staged the concert, Adam Yauch said: "I tried to imagine New York being taken over, my friends and family imprisoned and tortured and buildings I knew being ripped down and having to leave and not being able to return, things like that. The film was mainly created to raise awareness amongst American young people. As for the participants, we tried to find people whose values are in line with what the Tibetan freedom struggle represents, but it also has to do with who is available." MCA also acknowledged that the documentary represented another step towards maturity for the Beastie Boys: "I learned a lot through the time around *Licensed To Ill*. It was fun but I think that slowly over the past ten years, I've learned a lot. We're raised with these ideas in the West through all our media that what's going to bring us happiness is fame, wealth and beautiful people to have sex with. After *Licensed To Ill*, we went through a lot of reflection to come to the idea that trying to do things that are positive is what brings a person true lasting happiness."

By the by, *Free Tibet*'s awesome army of cinematographers includes band photographer Ricky Powell plus Beastie affiliate Spike Jonze and his brother-in-law, Roman 'son of Francis Ford' Coppola. 4/5

Alive

The Beastie Boys On-Stage Experience

From gigging in front of handfuls of mates in New York lofts to playing in the round at Wembley Arena – nothing better symbolises the Beastie Boys' rise to high estate than their growth as a live act.

Quite what those early gigs were like, we can only guess. However, if you can imagine a four-piece band playing at a party at your mate's cramped flat, you're probably in the right ballpark. Okay, so there might have been more pot, drink and/or swearing than at your regular shindig, but we're still talking about an experience that's a long way from all-seater stadia.

Of course, the boys did get the chance to play arenas when they supported Madonna on the Virgin Tour although I'd hesitate to talk about those as bona fide Beastie Boys gigs since i) the audience were obviously there to see Ms Ciccone ii) the boys weren't meant to be on the tour being, in fact, late replacements for The Fat Boys and iii) the group spent about as much time entertaining/antagonising the crowd as they did trying to persuade the promoters not to fire them for their on- and off-stage horseplay. More relevant although not necessarily more inspired were the boys' concerts at infamous New York venues like CBGBs. The nature of these gigs can best be measured by checking out the episode of *Rock Family Trees* that examines the New York punk scene in which The Ramones and Debbie Harry sentimentalise about playing a cramped basement with a toilet that makes the one in Danny Boyle's *Trainspotting* look like the facilities at the Savoy. Alternatively, you could just go and take a look at one of the wannabe bands playing at Covent Garden's Rock Garden venue. For all the hype and history, CBGBs is a decidedly average venue and, therefore, a rather appropriate place for the early, not-very-good-incarnation of the Beastie Boys to perform at.

As *Licensed To Ill* kicked things off for the band chartwise so touring the album was the making of the group as a live act. *The Village Voice*'s Joe Levy had this to say about the Beasties' mid- to late 1980s live experience: 'They wanted to be the loudest, meanest, baddest motherfuckers on the face of the earth. They wanted to drink from the biggest bottle of beer and wave around the biggest gun.' Unable to find a howitzer and a silo-sized bottle of Bud, the boys instead took to stages accompanied by caged go-go dancers, crates of lager and an 18-foot-long hydraulic penis. With such paraphernalia there was little chance of the band being upstaged – in the US, support act and Def Jam label mates Public Enemy did once manage to outdo the Beasties by going on stage brandishing fake Uzis.

Levy's other observation, that the band was 'fast and loose with their mouths,' smacks of understatement. Of the Beasties' many social faux pas, their gravest took place during a concert at Liverpool. As actor Simon O'Brien (aka Damon Grant from *Brookside*) recalled on BBC2's *I Love 1987*: "They came on stage and said: 'Hey, Liverpool, we hear you're bad. But we're the Beastie Boys and we're badder.' And we were like: 'Woo hoo! Riot!'" As fury erupted on the Mersey, the group panicked, rushing off stage only to return wielding baseball bats. It was during the ensuing melee that Adam Horovitz was accused of striking a girl in the face with a beer can he'd thrown into the audience with his Louisville Slugger. Adrock wound up in court and, although, he would eventually win the case, his arrest meant the Japanese leg of the Beasties' world tour had to be briefly postponed.

The Raising Hell tour left the Beastie Boys severely chastened. Rick Rubin: "I remember talking to Mike and Adam Horovitz. I was so excited about how great it was that all of this good and/or bad stuff was going on – this for a new band. And I remember them saying that it's different when you're actually doing it as opposed to reading about it. Going out and having people hate you is a very hard thing and it came very close to breaking the band up." Little wonder, then, that after touring the States for a second time with Run DMC, the Beastie Boys chose not to play live again for the best part of four years.

When the band did initially get back on the road it was to play small venues like London's Rough Trade record shop and the Marquee. However, while they didn't tour *Paul's Boutique* at all (the band's reluctance to perform was only marginally greater than that of Capitol Record's who refused to promote what they considered an unsellable album), the group found the courage to play global dates to promote *Check Your Head* which was no bad thing since, after both it and *Ill Communication* blew up, you would have had to be either a fool or a communist not to try and cash in on the success with a few stadium gigs. The two LPs were, in fact, so massive the group wound up playing everywhere from Nagoya to Neath and became a regular fixture on the Loolapalooza circuit in the US.

Unfortunately, I wasn't able to catch up with the boys during this period since I was living in America at the time they visited Britain and had returned home before they set foot back in the States. I did, however, catch a performance of 'Sabotage' on *The Late Show With David Letterman*, the sheer roof-raising force of which leads me to conclude that seeing the Beasties live in the early to mid-1990s must have been a pretty sublime experience.

TV appearances have actually been a strong point of the band for some time. They're particularly good at stealing the MTV Video Music Awards from under the noses of bands with much bigger budgets and much better looks. The 1998 VMAs were a case in point. While other acts phoned in workmanlike renditions of hit songs, the Beasties gave the punters something fresh. Introduced by an obviously very excited Ben Stiller ("Ladies and gentlemen – BEASTIE BOYS!"), the trio trotted on stage in their orange boiler suits and set about a breathtaking rendition of 'Three MCs And One DJ.' Marvellously backed by Mix Master Mike, the group whipped the audience of celebs into a near frenzy. Honestly, you haven't seen so many excited people since they held random drugs testing at the Oscars. Then, just as it looked like they didn't have anywhere else to go, the boys inquired: "Mix Master Mike, what ya gotta say?," the DJ hit a switch, the opening beats of 'Intergalactic' rang out and the band delivered an inspired version of their smash hit single, complete with fresh beats and kooky dance moves. By comparison, Will Smith teaming up with Dru Hill's Sisqo and Stevie Wonder looked like the midnight cabaret at Minehead Butlins.

If the VMAs had shown that the Beasties could still tear up the house, the Tibetan Freedom Concerts proved that the group could not only look credible in orange jump suits but were big enough to headline gigs featuring the likes of R.E.M., the Red Hot Chili Peppers, Radiohead, Foo Fighters, Bjork and Blur. The boys' charity turns were so great, in fact, that when it was announced that the band would tour the world to promote *Hello Nasty*, the tickets couldn't have sold out quicker if they'd been coated in crack. What made these concerts particularly memorable was that the band had decided to play in the round. Artists have traditionally preferred to face audiences head-on since it reduces the chances of feeling exposed. Perhaps thinking that they'd licked conventional performing, the Beasties went out on a limb, the end product of which was some of the greatest gigs of the late twentieth century. Initially taking to the stage with just Mix Master Mike for company, the Beasties would bring on other musicians throughout the act, including Money Mark, until by the time it came to close proceedings with 'Sabotage,' there was a full band performing. And just how did this bunch of average-looking blokes hold audiences spellbound from Glasgow to Greensboro, Ohio? Laser shows? Fancy choreography? Nope – they did it by playing some killer tunes, sporting some rather fetching grey shirts and throwing some funky martial arts-style shapes. Truth be told, the Beasties dance in a pretty geeky fashion but this reflects one of their central messages – looking cool counts for nothing, so be true to yourself and you can't go wrong. Even if this means boogieing like an epileptic Bruce Lee.

More recently, a US tour co-headlining with Rage Against The Machine had to be cancelled firstly because Mike D injured his shoulder falling off a mountain bike and secondly because Zac De La Rocha's outfit split up. Since that time, the only gigs the group have played have been in support of the Milarepa-backed New Yorkers Against Violence Fund (see Another Direction?). When and if the Beastie Boys do return to full-time touring, their concerts will have a rather different feel as Adrock explained at the 1999 MTV Music Video Awards: "I read in the news and heard from my friends all about the sexual assaults that went down at Woodstock '99. And it made me feel really sad and angry. I was thinking why should I just feel mad about it and not do anything about it? I think we can do something about it as musicians. I think we can talk to the promoters and make sure they're doing something about the safety of all the girls and the women that come to our shows. I think we can talk and work with the security people to make sure they know and understand about sexual harassment and rape and they know how to handle these situations."

Extracurricular Activities

Given their tendency to go on hiatus for years at a time, it won't surprise you to learn that the Beasties have been able to fit a few collaborations into their hectic work schedules. The first member of the band to get it together with another artist was MCA who hooked up with Burzootie to form Drum Machine before the Beasties had even recorded a track for Def Jam. Yauch has since forged an interesting side business supplying his bass skills (both slap and stand-up) to bands like Nighty-9 and Abstract Rude. Diamond and Horovitz have also performed on other artists' tracks, Mike D thumping the tubs for Grand Royal signing Ben Lee and Adrock playing bass on the DFL album *My Crazy Life*. Adam H also founded his own project band, BS 2000, about whom the kindest thing that can be said is that the collapse of Grand Royal means they're now without a label.

Rather more impressive is the group's freelance remixing work. Diamond has been particularly prolific in this field, tinkering with tracks by Moby ('Natural Blues'), Bjork ('Army Of Me'), Ween ('Spirit Of '76') and The Jon Spencer Blues Explosion ('Flavor (Part 1)' – Part 2 was reworked by Beck, incidentally). As for his bandmates, Yauch produced the Big Fat Love LP *Hellhouse* for ex-Beastie John Berry (Mike D played drums on the record) and worked over the Yoko Ono number 'The Source' while Adrock tweaked the knobs on band associate DJ Hurricane's album track 'Japanese Eyes.'

Although the boys clearly have a lot of fun in the booth and playing back-up, it's when they sing on other groups' numbers that they really soar. So be sure to check out Mike and Adam H's fabulous rhyming on 'Squat' from the De La Soul album *Art Official Intelligence I: Mosaic Thump*. And while Mike's styling on 'The Knock: Drums Of Death Part II' on the UNKLE LP *Psyence Fiction* relies rather too much on his previous work (the opening of the second verse is just the beginning of 'Paul Revere' reheated), the way project leader DJ Shadow samples Diamond's voice on 'UNKLE <Main Title Theme>' is as ingenious as it is effective.

Grand Royal: A Divine Madness

Taking its name from a slogan the group had been banding about since *Licensed To Ill* (those seeking fan information were directed to an address beginning 'Grand Royal – Guaranteed Fresh') and using as its insignia a pair of die and an unbeatable poker hand, Grand Royal was either a shoddily run corporation or the Beastie Boys' most awesome indulgence, depending upon your point of view.

Initially, Grand Royal simply provided the boys with a means of releasing their own material without massive amounts of interference from their parent label, Capitol. When *Check Your Head* (a joint Capitol Records/ Grand Royal venture like all the band's later albums) became an unexpected hit, the group was given a license to sign up and distribute material by other acts. Since they'd always placed a lot of importance in loyalty, the band made their first approach to one time Beastie Girl Kate Schellenbach. The boys have never really commented upon Schellenbach's decision to quit the band, although given the shame they now exhibit about their sexist past, it's fair to suggest that they probably aren't too proud about the fact that the band's sole female member felt so marginalised, she felt there was nothing left for her to do except leave. By signing up Schellenbach's new act Luscious Jackson whose *In Search Of Manny* would become Grand Royal's first non-Beastie release, Yauch, Horovitz and Diamond revealed both the extent to which they had evolved and their new found desire to act in a positive manner wherever possible.

Luscious Jackson would go on to become the second most successful Grand Royal outfit, scoring hit singles, contributing to the soundtrack of the movie *Clueless* and making an advert for the Gap chain. Other Grand Royal signings fared less well. John and Yoko's son Sean Lennon, Britain's Bis (whose high point was being chosen as Radio One DJ Simon Mayo's record of the week), Ben Lee… that you might not have heard of them has a lot to do with the fact these acts couldn't have had a hit if they'd made a pact with the Devil.

In truth, a lot of what came out on Grand Royal records was unspeakable garbage. There were a few great releases (At The Drive-In's *Relationship Of Command* came within a whisker of beating out the Fun Lovin' Criminals' *Loco* for *Ralph* magazine's album of 2001 award) and some notable near misses (i.e. the Beasties picking up well thought-of German act Atari Teenage Riot and arranging for their heroes Bad Brains to record an LP only for both groups to bugger off to bigger labels). For the most part, however, Grand Royal was synonymous with the sort of music you'd walk across motorways to avoid hearing.

Not that the poor quality of Grand Royal's output seemed to bother the Beastie Boys much. On the contrary, the group seemed to get off on the fact that they could make whatever deal they wanted and pump out whatever sort of fucked-up beats they desired. With Mike D as President, Adrock as head of A&R and MCA as Treasurer, the boys ran Grand Royal in the same way that Anthony H Wilson ran Manchester's Factory Records. They didn't have a master plan and, thanks to their personal success, weren't hamstrung by commercial concerns. They just did what they pleased, when they pleased. They were very pleased.

Grand Royal also became an occasional magazine. Ex-*Spin* magazine journo Bob Mack, whose pop at the boys' basketball skills had resulted in a rebuke on *Check Your Head*-era B-side 'Skills To Pay The Bills,' was originally hired to edit the most periodical of periodicals (it came out about as often as an agoraphobic) whose idiosyncratic content included profiles of the largely unheard-of Lee 'Scratch' Perry, complete histories of trainer manufacturers such as Nike and Adidas and incredibly long articles on X-treme sports like snowboarding, stock car racing and, er, golf. Imagine what skateboarding-and-youth-rebellion mag *Phat* might have been like had journo Gavin Hills had a chance to develop it beyond three issues or the sort of periodical *Loaded* would resemble if it contained fewer tits and more stuff on roller derbies and you'll have an idea of what kind of read *Grand Royal* was and why it sold so well.

Then again, the success of the magazine might have been down entirely to its pillorying of the mighty mullet. The haircut favoured by everyone from 'Achy Breaky Heart' auteur Billy Ray Cyrus to cricketing legend Ian Botham had long been a favourite of the Beasties who'd paid 'tribute' to its tonsorial excellence on the *Ill Communication*-era track 'Mullet Head' (refrain: 'Cut the sides, don't touch the back'). *Grand Royal* also made a big deal about the infamous hairdo so inspiring the Barney Hoskyns/Mark Larson best-selling hardback *The Mullet: Haircut Of The Gods* and Michael

Swindle's *Mulletheads : The Legends, Lore, Magic, And Mania Surrounding The Humble But Celebrated Mullet.*

Under Mike D's aegis, Grand Royal also dabbled in online radio and the world of fashion. The sort of T-shirts commissioned by clothing offshoot X-Large didn't feature yer standard band logos, though. Such are the weird ways of the Beasties, you were as likely to find clothes carrying the 'Aloha Mr Hand' catchphrase of Jeff Spicoli, the arch-stoner played by Sean Penn in the Cameron Crowe-scripted *Fast Times At Ridgemont High*, as you were bearing the name of either the band or its members.

With its odd signings, mind-boggling magazine and 'interesting' merchandise, Grand Royal seems in some ways to have been modelled on The Beatles' Apple experiment, although the Beasties being the Beasties the whole thing came off rather more like The Rutles' money leaking operation Rutle Corp. Of course, the insanity couldn't go on forever and Grand Royal finally ceased trading in the Autumn of 2001. "This is one of the most difficult decisions we've ever had to make," Mike D said at the time. "Over the years, the Grand Royal family had grown to include some of the most talented musicians and staff in the business. It's tragic that the same growth has also produced an overhead and infrastructure that is no longer viable."

While it's easy to love the idea of Grand Royal, it's difficult to admire much of what it produced. The organisation's highs and lows were perhaps best summed up by *Q* magazine who gave the boys props for lording the mullet, giving Spike Jonze free reign and discovering the aforementioned At The Drive-In but savaged them for their obsession with stock car racing and inflicting Adrock's BS 2000 upon an undeserving world. In the end, the real problem was that Grand Royal's output was the antithesis of the Beastie Boys' music – the experiments were rarely successful and what was produced was seldom essential.

The collapse of Grand Royal represented the Beastie Boys' first out and out failure since record buyers overlooked *Paul's Boutique* a decade earlier. For the first time in a long time, our heroes seemed fallible, their future uncertain...

Another Direction?

So, there you have it – the greatest story ever told. Other than the one about Jesus, obviously.

2002 actually finds the Beastie Boys at something of a crossroads. Four years on from the release of *Hello Nasty*, there's still no word on when the group's next album is due out – it's not even known if the boys are working on any fresh material. The collapse of Grand Royal, meanwhile, is symbolic of the fact that even the certain things in the band's universe have come unstuck. With both Mike Diamond and Adam Horovitz having recently split from their partners and Adam Yauch having been forced to cancel a Tibetan Freedom Concert in London in the summer of 2001 at the last minute, it's hard to imagine how things could be any worse for the boys.

Even in these testing times, the group continues to defy both authority and the odds. No sooner had George W Bush announced that he was to wage war on Alaska in his quest for precious, precious oil than Mike D published a stinging rebuke on the band's Website: 'President Bush's energy plan recommends drilling for oil in the biological heart of the Arctic National Wildlife Refuge, bringing back nuclear power, cutting research spending on alternative energy and basically causing irreversible damage to the planet, heading us back to a time when humanoids dragged their knuckles on the ground.' And in the fallout from September 11, while the rest of America was (with some justice, perhaps) baying for justice and revenge, the boys organised two New Yorkers For Peace concerts, designed to raise money for the victims of the World Trade Center attacks but to also promote an atmosphere of tolerance and understanding. As Mike D explained: "In light of everything New York City's firefighters, police and rescue workers have already done, getting this event together is the least we could do. The sacrifices and true heroics of these people have been an inspiration to the entire world. It is the greatest hope of the organisers and artists involved that the New York community will join in uniting against violence in all its forms, while providing assistance to their neighbours." Featuring (amongst others) The Jon Spencer Blues Explosion, ace rapper Mos Def, the awesome Afrika Bambaataa and the boys themselves, the gigs raised over $100,000 – a staggering amount if you consider the lengths the group went to to distance themselves from the brand of super patriotism that was threatening to engulf America at the time.

And it is this that makes the Beastie Boys truly amazing – this ability to constantly play by their own rules, to do what they think is right rather than commercially viable. Divorce, deceased record labels, a shortage of new material – sure, the Beastie Boys seem to have their backs against the wall but my money's on them to come out fighting. Isn't yours?

STOP PRESS – Just prior to this book going to print, *Rolling Stone* ran a story that the Beastie Boys were about to start recording their sixth LP proper. "We're currently at the incubation stage," claimed Mix Master Mike. "We've got all the beats in the incubator. They're eggs. We're waiting for them to hatch." Given the boys' past form, we can expect the new record any time within the next five years. Me? I'm getting excited already!

Discography

A fully comprehensive Beastie Boys' singles and EPs discography would run the length of this book. Angus Batey's book tries to catalogue the group's complete works but I'm sure that, despite his very best efforts, he'd agree that he wasn't able to cover all the bases. In lieu of this, here's the band's full UK singles chart history.

'(You Gotta) Fight For Your Right (To Party)' [Def Jam 650418 7] – released on 28 February 1987, it was on the chart for 11 weeks and peaked at number 11.

'No Sleep Till Brooklyn' [Def Jam BEAST 1] – released on 30 May 1987, it stayed on the chart for seven weeks, with a highest position of 14.

'She's On It' [Def Jam BEAST 2] – came out on 18 July 1987 and reached number 10, staying on the chart for eight weeks.

'Girls'/'She's Crafty' [Def Jam BEAST 3] – this double A-side was released on 3 October 1987 and peaked at number 34. It stayed on the survey for just four weeks.

'Pass The Mic' [Capitol 12CL 653] – released on 11 April 1992, over five years after the group's last chart hit. It remained on the chart for just two weeks and peaked at number 47.

'Frozen Metal Head' [Capitol 12CL 665] – this EP was released on 4 July 1992. It stayed on the chart for just one week, reaching number 55 in the process. The tracks featured on the record were 'Jimmy James,' 'Jimmy James (Original),' 'Drinkin' Wine' and 'The Blue Nun.'

'Get It Together'/'Sabotage' [Capitol CDCL 716] – another double A-side, this was issued on 9 July 1994. On the survey for four weeks, it reached number 19, making it the group's first top 20 hit for six years.

'Sure Shot' [Capitol CDCLS 726] – released on 26 November 1994, it peaked at number 27 and stayed on chart for just three weeks.

'Intergalactic' [Grand Royal CDCL 803] – issued on Independence Day 1998, 'Intergalactic' was on the chart for seven weeks and peaked at number five, making it the Beasties' second top 10 single and their biggest chart hit today.

'Body Movin'' [Grand Royal CDCLS 809] – The Norman 'Fatboy Slim' Cook remix of the *Hello Nasty* album track came out on 7 November 1998 and reached number 15.

'Remote Control'/'Three MCs & One DJ' [Grand Royal CDCL 812] – The latest in a series of double A-sides, this was released on 29 May 1999 and reached number 21. It remained on chart for three weeks.

'Alive' [Grand Royal CDCL 818] – Issued on 18 December 1999, the single stalled at number 28 and was on the survey for four weeks.

Resource Materials

Books

It's quite amazing that, despite the Beastie Boys' impressive record sales and immeasurable influence, there are only four books on the band (apart from this one) currently on the market and, of these, only the first mentioned is truly essential.

Rhyming & Stealing: A History Of The Beastie Boys by Angus Batey, 1998, Independent Music Press, GB, 208 pages, £9.99, ISBN: 1897783140. It's hard to say enough good things about Angus' book. Imagine a well-informed text written by a fan who has actually encountered his heroes and you're getting somewhere near to the mark. With interesting insights into the origins of hip hop and the boys' extracurricular activities there really isn't a lot of ground left uncovered. And if the writing itself isn't brilliant enough, the reference section and in particular the discography is a work of thoroughly researched genius. Incidentally, when I met Angus, he told me that he'd actually been able to give a copy of *Rhyming & Stealing* to the band when he went behind the scenes at one of their US concerts. According to the author, he handed the book to Mike D whose first response was to ask whether there was anything he should be worried about legally. When Angus reassured him there wasn't, Diamond replied: "Well, congratulations, I guess." Pop stars, eh? Is there anyone more difficult to impress?

The Beastie Boys by Michael Heatley, 1999, Omnibus Press, GB, 95 pages, £8.95, ISBN: 0711976368. An okay text but nothing to get particularly excited about. Like the rest of the Omnibus series, it's a pretty perfunctory piece. Only the overall shortage of info on the band makes this a worthwhile purchase.

The Beastie Boys Companion by John Rocco, 2000, Schirmer Press, US, 200 pages, £9.95, ISBN: 0825671590. Quite simply, not a very good book. Shit, you wouldn't mete out shoddy treatment like this to S Club Seven. Well, maybe you would...

Pass The Mic – The Beastie Boys 1991 – 1996 by Avi Marcopolous, 2001, Powerhouse Books, US, 144 pages, £45.00, ISBN: 1576871088. Great photos can't justify the exorbitant asking price.

Video

There aren't actually any Beastie Boys videos on the market at the moment. The following have all been deleted but you might still be able to find copies in specialist stores and second-hand shops.

The Beastie Boys Video
Sabotage Video
The Skills to Pay The Bills Video

DVD

There's only one B-Boy DVD available but it's so damn definitive, you'll never need another. All the promos plus a wealth of bonus information: trust me, in the future all music DVDs will be like...

Beastie Boys Video Anthology (4924239)

On The Web

As a band that's always looked to the future, it's no surprise to find that the Beastie Boys have a number of well-kept rest areas on the Information Superhighway. Here's a list of the five finest Beastie sites.

Beastie Boys – Welcome to Planet Beastie. Latest news, press releases, lyrics, an awesome discography, the boys' own take on their unlikely rise to power – this is the equivalent of a superhighway one-stop shop. http://www.beastieboys.com/

Beastie Boys Direct – So what, so what, so what'cha want? It doesn't matter thanks to this superb site which has been specially designed to meet all your Beastie merchandising requirements. http://www.beastieboysdirect.com/

Beastie Boys 411 – A site that stands out courtesy of its impressive picture archive (if you need proof of how bad the boys are at basketball, look no further), its thorough band history (lifted from sonicnet.com) and a superb selection of Real Audio files, the highlight being a version of 'So What'cha Want' on which the Beasties duet with Cypress Hill. Could do with more regular updating, however. http://www.think-ahead.nl/BeastieBoys/news.htm

Beastie Boys Mother Ship – A wing of the very wonderful Inkblot online magazine that's awash with info, opinion and insight. http://www.inkblotmagazine.com/beastie_mothership.htm

The Beastie Shrine – Gives the boys' official site a run for its money thanks to its quite incredible interview archive – if you can't find it here, it's safe to assume that the Beasties didn't say it. The site is also home to a discography so complete, it will enable you to track down those rare live recordings and Nagorno Karabakh 12-inch singles you've long sought. http://beastieshrine.isontheweb.com.

The Essential Library: History Best-Sellers

Build up your library with new titles published every month

Conspiracy Theories by Robin Ramsay, £3.99

Do you think *The X-Files* is fiction? That Elvis is dead? That the US actually went to the moon? And don't know that the ruling elite did a deal with the extra-terrestrials after the Roswell crash in 1947... At one time, you could blame the world's troubles on the Masons or the Illuminati, or the Jews, or One Worlders, or the Great Communist Conspiracy. Now we also have the alien-US elite conspiracy, or the alien shape-shifting reptile conspiracy to worry about - and there are books to prove it as well! This book tries to sort out the handful of wheat from the choking clouds of intellectual chaff. For among the nonsensical Conspiracy Theory rubbish currently proliferating on the Internet, there are important nuggets of real research about real conspiracies waiting to be mined.

The Rise Of New Labour by Robin Ramsay, £3.99

The rise of New Labour? How did that happen? As everybody knows, Labour messed up the economy in the 1970s, went too far to the left, became 'unelectable' and let Mrs Thatcher in. After three General Election defeats Labour modernised, abandoned the left and had successive landslide victories in 1997 and 2001.

That's the story they print in newspapers. The only problem is...the real story of the rise of New Labour is more complex, and it involves the British and American intelligence services, the Israelis and elite management groups like the Bilderbergers.

Robin Ramsay untangles the myths and shows how it really happened that Gordon Brown sank gratefully into the arms of the bankers, Labour took on board the agenda of the City of London, and that nice Mr Blair embraced his role as the last dribble of Thatcherism down the leg of British politics.

UFOs by Neil Nixon, £3.99

UFOs and Aliens have been reported throughout recorded time. Reports of UFO incidents vary from lights in the sky to abductions. The details are frequently terrifying, always baffling and occasionally hilarious. This book includes the best known cases, the most incredible stories and the answers that explain them. There are astounding and cautionary tales which suggest that the answers we seek may be found in the least likely places.

The Essential Library: History Best-Sellers

Build up your library with new titles published every month

Ancient Greece by Mike Paine, £3.99

Western civilization began with the Greeks. From the highpoint of the 5th century BC through the cultural triumphs of the Alexandrian era to their impact on the developing Roman empire, the Greeks shaped the philosophy, art, architecture and literature of the Mediterranean world. Mike Paine provides a concise and well-informed narrative of many centuries of Greek history. He highlights the careers of great political and military leaders like Pericles and Alexander the Great, and shows the importance of the great philosophers like Plato and Aristotle. Dramatists and demagogues, stoics and epicureans, aristocrats and helots take their places in the unfolding story of the Greek achievement.

Black Death by Sean Martin, £3.99

The Black Death is the name most commonly given to the pandemic of bubonic plague that ravaged the medieval world in the late 1340s. From Central Asia the plague swept through Europe, leaving millions of dead in its wake. Between a quarter and a third of Europe's population died. In England the population fell from nearly six million to just over three million. The Black Death was the greatest demographic disaster in European history.

American Civil War by Phil Davies, £3.99

The American Civil War, fought between North and South in the years 1861-1865, was the bloodiest and most traumatic war in American history. Rival visions of the future of the United States faced one another across the battlefields and families and friends were bitterly divided by the conflict. This book examines the deep-rooted causes of the war, so much more complicated than the simple issue of slavery.

American Indian Wars by Howard Hughes, £3.99

At the beginning of the 1840s the proud tribes of the North American Indians looked across the plains at the seemingly unstoppable expansion of the white man's West. During the decades of conflict that followed, as the new world pushed onward, the Indians saw their way of life disappear before their eyes. Over the next 40 years they clung to a dream of freedom and a continuation of their traditions, a dream that was repeatedly shattered by the whites.

The Essential Library: Film Best-Sellers

Build up your library with new titles every month

Film Noir by Paul Duncan

The laconic private eye, the corrupt cop, the heist that goes wrong, the femme fatale with the rich husband and the dim lover - these are the trademark characters of Film Noir. This book charts the progression of the Noir style as a vehicle for film-makers who wanted to record the darkness at the heart of American society as it emerged from World War to the Cold War. As well as an introduction explaining the origins of Film Noir, seven films are examined in detail and an exhaustive list of over 500 Films Noirs are listed.

Alfred Hitchcock by Paul Duncan

More than 20 years after his death, Alfred Hitchcock is still a household name, most people in the Western world have seen at least one of his films, and he popularised the action movie format we see every week on the cinema screen. He was both a great artist and dynamite at the box office. This book examines the genius and enduring popularity of one of the most influential figures in the history of the cinema!

Orson Welles by Martin Fitzgerald

The popular myth is that after the artistic success of *Citizen Kane* it all went downhill for Orson Welles, that he was some kind of fallen genius. Yet, despite overwhelming odds, he went on to make great Films Noirs like *The Lady From Shanghai* and *Touch Of Evil*. He translated Shakespeare's work into films with heart and soul (*Othello, Chimes At Midnight, Macbeth*), and he gave voice to bitterness, regret and desperation in *The Magnificent Ambersons* and *The Trial*. Far from being down and out, Welles became one of the first cutting-edge independent film-makers.

Woody Allen (Revised & Updated Edition) by Martin Fitzgerald

Woody Allen: Neurotic. Jewish. Funny. Inept. Loser. A man with problems. Or so you would think from the characters he plays in his movies. But hold on. Allen has written and directed 30 films. He may be a funny man, but he is also one of the most serious American film-makers of his generation. This revised and updated edition includes *Sweet And Lowdown* and *Small Time Crooks*.

Stanley Kubrick by Paul Duncan

Kubrick's work, like all masterpieces, has a timeless quality. His vision is so complete, the detail so meticulous, that you believe you are in a three-dimensional space displayed on a two-dimensional screen. He was commercially successful because he embraced traditional genres like War (*Paths Of Glory, Full Metal Jacket*), Crime (*The Killing*), Science Fiction (*2001*), Horror (*The Shining*) and Love (*Barry Lyndon*). At the same time, he stretched the boundaries of film with controversial themes: underage sex (*Lolita*); ultra violence (*A Clockwork Orange*); and erotica (*Eyes Wide Shut*).

94

The Essential Library: Recent Film Releases

Build up your library with new titles every month

Tim Burton by Colin Odell & Michelle Le Blanc

Tim Burton makes films about outsiders on the periphery of society. His heroes are psychologically scarred, perpetually naive and childlike, misunderstood or unintentionally disruptive. They upset convential society and morality. Even his villains are rarely without merit - circumstance blurs the divide between moral fortitude and personal action. But most of all, his films have an aura of the fairytale, the fantastical and the magical.

French New Wave by Chris Wiegand

The directors of the French New Wave were the original film geeks - a collection of celluloid-crazed cinéphiles with a background in film criticism and a love for American auteurs. Having spent countless hours slumped in Parisian cinémathèques, they armed themselves with handheld cameras, rejected conventions, and successfully moved movies out of the studios and on to the streets at the end of the 1950s.

Borrowing liberally from the varied traditions of film noir, musicals and science fiction, they released a string of innovative and influential pictures, including the classics *Jules Et Jim* and *A Bout De Souffle*. By the mid-1960s, the likes of Jean-Luc Godard, François Truffaut, Claude Chabrol, Louis Malle, Eric Rohmer and Alain Resnais had changed the rules of film-making forever.

Bollywood by Ashok Banker

Bombay's prolific Hindi-language film industry is more than just a giant entertainment juggernaut for 1 billion-plus Indians worldwide. It's a part of Indian culture, language, fashion and lifestyle. It's also a great bundle of contradictions and contrasts, like India itself. Thrillers, horror, murder mysteries, courtroom dramas, Hong Kong-style action gunfests, romantic comedies, soap operas, mythological costume dramas... they're all blended with surprising skill into the musical boy-meets-girl formula of Bollywood. This vivid introduction to Bollywood, written by a Bollywood scriptwriter and media commentator, examines 50 major films in entertaining and intimate detail.

Mike Hodges by Mark Adams

Features an extensive interview with Mike Hodges. His first film, *Get Carter*, has achieved cult status (recently voted the best British film ever in *Hotdog* magazine) and continues to be the benchmark by which every British crime film is measured. His latest film, *Croupier*, was such a hit in the US that is was re-issued in the UK. His work includes crime drama (*Pulp*), science-fiction (*Flash Gordon* and *The Terminal Man*), comedy (*Morons From Outer Space*) and watchable oddities such as *A Prayer For The Dying* and *Black Rainbow*. Mike Hodges is one of the great maverick British filmmakers.

The Essential Library: Currently Available

Film Directors:

Woody Allen (2nd)	**Tim Burton**	**Ang Lee**
Jane Campion*	**John Carpenter**	**Joel & Ethan Coen (2nd)**
Jackie Chan	**Steven Soderbergh**	**Clint Eastwood**
David Cronenberg	**Terry Gilliam***	**Michael Mann**
Alfred Hitchcock (2nd)	**Krzysztof Kieslowski***	**Roman Polanski**
Stanley Kubrick (2nd)	**Sergio Leone**	**Oliver Stone**
David Lynch	**Brian De Palma***	**George Lucas**
Sam Peckinpah*	**Ridley Scott (2nd)**	**James Cameron**
Orson Welles (2nd)	**Billy Wilder**	
Steven Spielberg	**Mike Hodges**	

Film Genres:

Blaxploitation Films	**Bollywood**	**French New Wave**
Horror Films	**Spaghetti Westerns**	**Vietnam War Movies**
Slasher Movies	**Film Noir**	**Hammer Films**
Vampire Films*	**Heroic Bloodshed***	**Carry On Films**
German Expressionist Films		

Film Subjects:

Laurel & Hardy	**Marx Brothers**	**Film Music**
Steve McQueen*	**Marilyn Monroe**	**The Oscars® (2nd)**
Filming On A Microbudget	**Bruce Lee**	**Writing A Screenplay**
Film Studies		

Music:

The Madchester Scene	**Beastie Boys**	**Jethro Tull**
How To Succeed In The Music Business		

Literature:

Cyberpunk	**Philip K Dick**	**The Beat Generation**
Agatha Christie	**Sherlock Holmes**	**Noir Fiction***
Terry Pratchett	**Hitchhiker's Guide (2nd)**	**Alan Moore**
William Shakespeare	**Creative Writing**	**Tintin**

Ideas:

Conspiracy Theories	**Nietzsche**	**UFOs**
Feminism	**Freud & Psychoanalysis**	**Bisexuality**

History:

Alchemy & Alchemists	**The Crusades**	**The Black Death**
Jack The Ripper	**The Rise Of New Labour**	**Ancient Greece**
American Civil War	**American Indian Wars**	**Witchcraft**
Globalisation	**Who Shot JFK?**	

Miscellaneous:

Stock Market Essentials	**How To Succeed As A Sports Agent**	**Doctor Who**

Available at bookstores or send a cheque (payable to 'Oldcastle Books') to: **Pocket Essentials (Dept BB), P O Box 394, Harpenden, Herts, AL5 1XJ, UK.** £3.99 each (£2.99 if marked with an *). For each book add 50p(UK)/£1 (elsewhere) postage & packing